D0857471

Crosscurrents / MODERN CRITIQUES

Harry T. Moore, *General Editor*

The Legacy of
VAN WYCK BROOKS
A Study
of Maladies and Motives

Willam Wasserstrom

WITH A PREFACE BY
Harry T. Moore

SOUTHERN ILLINOIS UNIVERSITY PRESS
Carbondale and Edwardsville

FEFFER & SIMONS, INC.
London and Amsterdam

To Rose

Contents

Preface

All of us who read about and think about American culture, particularly in relation to its literature, owe a massive debt to Van Wyck Brooks. William Wasserstrom says this in the present volume, which is nevertheless fairly critical. Fairly is used here in a double sense, meaning justly as well as amply.

Mr. Wasserstrom has definitely not written a biography of Brooks, as he makes plain in his Introduction; but, as he points out, there are ample materials for such a volume in some of Brooks's own work and in the excellent memoir by his widow. There are also unpublished papers, some of which Mr. Wasserstrom has usefully included in the present book. But a biography will certainly appear: already, Brooks's good friend Lewis Mumford has invited a brilliant woman novelist and essayist to write it, but like so many authors she has too many contractual obligations to undertake the project.

Brooks, incidentally, had been working on a biography of Lewis Mumford when his own death occurred in 1963. Also incidentally, Dutton has recently brought out the Mumford-Brooks correspondence, edited by Robert Spiller. Brooks, some years older than Mumford, was the pioneer in American-culture studies, and the young Lewis Mumford was the first really important writer to rally to the cause, with his books of the 1920s such as The Golden Day and Herman Melville. Then Mumford grew into a writer who dealt with international themes, particulary in relation to the history of cities; stemming from his youthful studies, his later books were prophetic in their warnings of pollution and of the perils of slum congestion, among many other subjects. Mumford indeed became a world writer of major proportions: it is preposterous that he—as well as Thornton Wilder, the late Robert Frost or, for that matter, the late Van Wyck Brooks—was never given the Nobel Prize instead of a Pearl Buck or a John Steinbeck.

Lewis Mumford's career provides a most interesting counterpoint to Van Wyck Brooks's. Their Letters show this in all its particularity. Indeed, the two men twice quarreled, in their own polite way, at the time when Mumford became a vital enemy of fascism in the 1930s and felt that Brooks wasn't giving himself sufficiently to that cause, and again when Brooks as chairman of an award-granting committee of the National Institute of Arts and Letters gave a medal to a pre-World War II isolationist. But the friendship between the two men was sturdy enough to outlast what sometimes appeared to be ideological differences; as Lewis Mumford has said, "If our friendship, however loving, never became deeply intimate, if some reserve and reticence always remained, we nonetheless could not part until death itself parted us."

Once again, this recent volume of their Letters shows the quite different range of their careers. Brooks stuck to American themes although, as Mr. Wasserstrom amply demonstrates, he was tempted by Europe, as Henry James, T. S. Eliot, Ezra Pound, and others were. Lewis Mumford spent a youthful year in Europe (see his short autobiographical novel, The Little Testament of Bernard Martin, reprinted in the collection of Mumford's work called The Human Prospect), and he has often revisited England and the Continent, but he has apparently never been tempted to become an expatriate despite the faults he has found with America; he is contented at his country home in New York State, where he is his own gardener, and during winter, he and his wife usually stay in Cambridge, Massachusetts, within range of Harvard.

Brooks, initiated early in life into the mystique of European travel, apparently ached to be an expatriate, but sternly set himself to the task of specializing on America. In 1920 he brought out The Ordeal of Mark Twain (revised 1933), which attempted to show how the natural gifts of the Missouri writer were hobbled by certain elements of American culture. Conversely, Brooks in The Pilgrimage of Henry James assayed to picture a man whose writings suffered because he had broken off most connections with his native land but was never able to sink roots in other countries.

Mr. Wasserstrom unfortunately doesn't give much space to that strange book and dismisses it rather cursorily. But he deals at length with Brooks's most ambitious effort, the five volumes of the Makers and Finders series. Like most critics above the middlebrow level, Mr. Wasserstrom doesn't rank these books very high, partly because he feels that their historical element spoils them; among other reasons it simplifies history into a kind of "fairy tale." If the Makers and Finders series is "a splendid achievement," it is also "a pernicious work." Mr. Wasserstrom joins most other critics in ultimately deploring the series, but asserts that the true importance of Brooks tends to be disregarded today. When he was "a radical critic, he imposed his stamp on two generations of reformist literary men, on Mumford, Waldo Frank, Matthew Josephson, Granville Hicks, Newton Arvin— above all on F. O. Mattiessen."

Mr. Wasserstrom looks carefully into the known facts of Brooks's breakdown in the twenties, which kept him from writing for several years. He emerged from the ordeal as from shadow into sunshine, with a more optimistic attitude to America's "usable" past (the term is his). The sections describing and analyzing all this is a compelling one. Mr. Wasserstrom ends his own part of the book with a reference to Lewis Mumford, as Brooks's successor, "the last Orphic voice of the twenties generation, as Brooks was in his time the first." I hope that "Orphic voice" metaphor is a well-meant one, for it must be said that Lewis Mumford is more than a mere voice, orphic or otherwise, for a now-fading generation; but there is no space for a discussion of his achievements here.

In the last part of this book, Mr. Wasserstrom presents some sixty pages of Brooks's own later writings (1960–63), chiefly introductions to books, prefatory essays which have not been collected before. These give us the latest thoughts of Brooks on a diverse series of American authors, including Stephen Crane, Fenimore Cooper, Washington Irving, and others, as well as such comparatively neglected writers as Harold Frederic and Robert Herrick, and a Chinese and a British author. But the emphasis is on American writers. Altogether, William Wasserstrom, in his own long bio-critical essay, and in making these Brooks essays available, has made a valuable contribution to a better understanding of the literature of the United States.

HARRY T. MOORE

Southern Illinois University
September 26, 1970

Acknowledgments

To the librarians and staffs at Harvard University, Syracuse University, Stanford University, Yale University, and The University of Pennsylvania, I am indebted; most particularly to Barbara Stokes Rees of the Charles Patterson Van Pelt Library at Pennsylvania, where the Van Wyck Brooks papers are held. To Mrs. Gladys Brooks, Malcolm Cowley, Lewis Mumford, and Robert E. Spiller I am grateful for hospitality of spirit as well as for the transmission of specific details of fact. The University of Minnesota Press has allowed me to draw on my essay, *Van Wyck Brooks*, published in its Minnesota Pamphlets on American Writers—to which I call attention both in its behalf and in my own behalf: *The Legacy of Van Wyck Brooks* introduces what I hope are recognized as alteration of tone and modification of fact. To Charles Van Wyck Brooks, who provided me with a bounty of letters written by his father during the latter's years of young manhood and who permitted me to publish these at will, I am most eager to record my thanks. A last word of gratitude is reserved for my son, Andy.

Introduction

The subtitle of this work does indeed describe its general drift. Although my essay includes a substantial amount of biographical matter, hitherto unpublished, is in part anecdotal and in some measure gossipy, it is by no means an account of the life of Van Wyck Brooks. The materials for a *Life* are in truth already in print, available in Mrs. Gladys Brooks's *If Strangers Meet* (1967) and in her husband's three volumes of autobiography, *Shadows and Portraits* (1954), *The Day of the Phoenix* (1957), and *From the Shadow of the Mountain* (1961). Interspersed among these books are occasional essays in self-explanation as well as whole volumes of self-clarification which serve to gloss the man's career— *Opinions of Oliver Allston* (1941), *The Writer in America* (1952), *A Writer's Notebook* (1958). From Brooks's own hand, therefore, we possess an unusually rich store of documents in memoir and reminiscence and, too, a plausible reason for their profusion. Brooks, who saw his career as a lifelong exercise in self-education, said that somehow he felt himself constrained to conduct his education in public. What this explanation does not encompass, however, what his memoirs do not offer is crucial. For Brooks deliberately or inadvertently failed to give his audience more than the tiniest glimpse of the connections between his thought and his need, between his character and his spirit, his judgment and his will, his passions and his mind—his education and his life. And it is the study of this ill-defined sphere, involving matters of peremptory interest for the investigation of men and ideas in our time, to which I have found myself drawn.

Inviting as this subject customarily is, it is peculiarly attractive as it bears on Brooks's achievement and reputation. For this extraordinarily gifted man sought to induce literary criticism to serve aims which are ordinarily reserved for fiction, hoped to assign personal memoir the role customarily performed by legend. My task has been therefore to retrace the designs of motive which led this half-historical, half-legendary figure to embrace certain portentous ideas, to initiate certain alliances, to exult in and to discredit particular modes of conducting the life of the mind in our time. Brooks's distinguishing feature was an ardor for thought. Salvation was his unalterable need. And his life was spent in an effort to reconcile his will and his want within the limits imposed by two literary disciplines, criticism and history, which are not remarkably well-adapted to fulfill these ends. A strange combination of daring and perversity of mind led him to think that he could compel these twin disciplines to serve as instruments of his will rather than as means for the study of the forms and patterns of the American imagination.

Now, nearly a decade after his death, a half century after he issued his first rallying call for reform of the intellectual life in America, he presents himself as one of the most engrossing figures of our recent past. Confronting Brooks, we contemplate the operation of a seismic intelligence whose energy once seemed to incarnate the temper of an entire literary generation, the twenties generation. Its chief survivors today are of course Glenway Wescott and Matthew Josephson, Granville Hicks, Malcolm Cowley and Kenneth Burke, Lewis Mumford and Edmund Wilson. Retracing Brooks's encounter with the social, political, moral and literary problems with which he and his colleagues were beset, we discover some traces of motive, not hidden merely unrecognized, within a group of distinguished persons—the very group, indeed, which cherished Brooks as its most unquenchably determined leader.

Despite vast differences of temperament and accomplishment, members of this group hang together—even today—by virtue of their disdain for the role of specialist of letters and by reason of their obstinate, Romantic faith in the grace and authority of the literary imagination. It is an incidental but impressive fact of the present moment that Mumford and Wilson, foremost members of that company, have engaged in a debate on precisely this subject with specialist scholars in *The New York Review of Books*, a debate which must be read as a *cri de coeur* of the twenties generation. Members of that vanishing race have not only resisted the technologizing of scholarship but too have continued to withstand the transfer of moral authority to the new men of social science.

Among the numberless sources of inspiration which shaped their styles of mind, Van Wyck Brooks preserves a signal place. For it was he who pressed his younger colleagues to regard all spheres of human nature and conduct as the proper concern of a literary intellectual in the United States. It was he, too, whose example dramatized and confirmed the power of eloquence and the uses of learning for the Tolstoyan task of proclaiming what must be done in America in order to nurture an authentic national literature. Unfortunately, he also displayed the ease with which a mind, absorbed so, might exchange the cutting edge of judgment for a bludgeon, might shift from praising nationalism to exalting regionalism.

That it was Van Wyck Brooks who took this route is itself a matter of wonder, a matter which presents a wonderful point of departure of an inquiry into those internal conflicts which underlay his decision. Even more compelling and poignant is the effort to understand why Brooks, whose private concerns expressed some general dilemmas, is undoubtedly the most profoundly representative figure of his age. The key problem of his own life was Europe. Enchanted by and absorbed in the romance of Europe, he forced himself to accept the crude but alterable fact of America, to inhabit and devote himself to a land that went against his grain. It was a brave and self-lacerating choice. And its pain can be properly gauged only when we recognize, at last, that in this respect he was not at all a man of the twentieth but was a man of the nineteenth century. He fought himself to a standstill over a problem of choice which had given his predecessors no trouble at all: they had found America simply uninhabitable. But in large degree because of Brooks's example, his followers and successors decided that the classic solution to the American dilemma—escape—could no longer serve. And as a result of that decision, today nearly unimaginable, a determined and resourceful man assumed the leadership of the nascent literary life in America.

It was an act and a role which came to him naturally but, as his subsequent life reveals, they were by no means natural. The exaltation of regionalism, a natural step in the order of Brooks's ideas, led to another step, the elevation, acclamation, and affirmation of a semimystic chauvinism. And Brooks, having reached this point at a certain moment in his career, found its lure too captivating to resist and found himself deposed as the reigning figure in American letters. To appraise the reasons why his followers abandoned him, to weigh the reasons for indifference today among younger critics, and perhaps to speak for those who continue to find themselves in his debt and thus to vindicate the man—this, in a word, is the burden of my essay.

WILLIAM WASSERSTROM

Briant's Neck, Massachusetts
September 7, 1970

The Legacy of Van Wyck Brooks
A Study of Maladies and Motives

Letter to Eleanor [Stimson]

Dear Eleanor

. . . I am going to tell you of a wild dream I had last night, the first I have had in a month: I thought . . . that my nature had split up into so many motives and furrows, which ran along quite independently that I had become incapable of any action or feeling which was absolutely whole-souled. Thus if one desire or feeling ran along one furrow, its opposite might run along the next. With this complexity you become confused and disgusted. Meanwhile a man came in whose mind was entirely trained in one channel: whose motives were consistent, and whose whole life was simple solutions. To my mind all his actions were puerile, because where he saw them from one point only, I (though incapable of performing them) weighed them from a hundred. Of everything that he did I would say: "How *simple*: but I would disdain to do anything so obvious." I was unable to perform the great complicated actions: the simple ones I despised; and consequently did nothing. There was a certain nobility in his simple actions: and you fell in love with him. Now see what the case was: nobility of heart is what one loves. I judged wholly of a man from his mind. My own mind, inconsistent and complicated, had destroyed my soul: so that to me the other man seemed ignoble. Thus feeling my own superiority of intellect, I was hurt again to think you cared more for him than for me, feeling as I did that I could prove him my inferior. It was wounded pride, among other disappointments. In this interesting state of affairs, I went off after him with a pistol (I only loved you now in a fierce mad way), and was just ending up by blowing out my own brains, when I woke up. . . .

Cambridge
Ever your loving friend,
Van Wyck

1

Less Than an Oracle

> When we think of the contempt for American authors,
> mixed with ignorance about them, that prevailed in the
> universities, during the reign of Barrett Wendell . . . we
> might also remember that Brooks had more to do with
> creating the new attitude than anyone else in the country.
> Not a few of the academic critics who attacked him in later
> years were men whose careers would have been impossible if
> Brooks had not found them a subject and broken a path
> they could follow.—Malcolm Cowley, 1963

"Who does not know the now routine legend in which the
world of 1910–1917 is Washington Square turned Arcadia,
in which the barriers are always down, the magazines always
promising, the workers always marching, geniuses sprouting
in every Village bedroom, Isadora Duncan always dancing—
that world of which John Reed was the Byronic hero, Mabel
Dodge the hostess, Randolph Bourne the martyr, Van Wyck
Brooks the oracle?" Amazing—that Alfred Kazin, in 1942,
exactly twenty-five years after the time which this synoptic
passage was intended to evoke, could assume as a matter of
course not only that the legend of national resurgence would
last indefinitely but also that the reputations of key persons
were unimpeachable. Today, after another twenty-five years,
that world appears more routine than miraculous. The
memory of Isadora fades. Bourne, the grief of his early
death mainly forgotten, regains only a modest attention.
Reed, chiefly by way of the fiftieth anniversary of the Soviet
Revolution, retains his brio indeed, but what of Mabel

1

Dodge? A period piece. And Brooks? Vanished—victim of history, perhaps, which is accustomed to a ceaseless exchange of oracles.

In the case of Brooks history has been wanton. His displacement from the center to the farthest margins of literary influence today is surely a stunning and, to anyone who came to maturity in America between the two world wars, incredible shift of taste. No single figure of our time, no man of letters, no intellectual in whatever sphere, academic or free lance, has acquired the kind of following or the sort of authority Brooks held in his heyday—as Edmund Wilson in 1924 caused Scott Fitzgerald to say in an "Imaginary Dialogue." Brooks called "a caustic role of the critics whom we found in authority," Fitzgerald observes—Paul Elmer More, Irving Babbitt, Stuart Pratt Sherman—then addressed our attention to the "boldness of the European masters" and finally "goaded us back to our place in the world. . . . You were almost alone, when you first began to write, in taking American literature seriously—in appraising it as rigorously as possible, in comparison with other literatures, and in exhorting us to better our achievements." High praise, indeed, whether it is attributed to Wilson or his persona.

Brooks's celebrity, then at its zenith, was the reward of work begun in 1908 with publication of *The Wine of the Puritans*, and enlarged during the next few years with those "delicate essays" in the study of a "wicked distemper" of spirit, as Paul Rosenfeld remarked, which held in thrall certain exquisite Continental and English men of letters to whom Brooks was then drawn—Senancour, Guérin, Amiel, John Addington Symonds. Although his fame had been blurred for a moment in 1914 because of an idiosyncratic study of H. G. Wells, by 1920 it was luminous and absolute. *America's Coming-of-Age, Letters and Leadership,* and *The Ordeal of Mark Twain* furnished the new generation of literary intellectuals with their first comprehensive vision of the effects of American moral, social, industrial, economic, sexual prejudices on American writing. Men marveled to hear disenchantment so enchantingly said. And they were persuaded that Brooks had genius of the kind he sought to commend in others, genius of the Whitmanesque, visionary, vatic kind.

These were some of the oracular ideas which Kazin assumed that everyone would associate with Brooks whose role, Mary Colum contended in her Dial Award essay, was comparable to that performed by the greatest men of letters in the entire history of human thought. No one blinked in disbelief and nearly everyone agreed with her judgment: if America had not yet produced an artist of the highest order of brilliance, it had acquired in Brooks a critic, faithful to one of the chief functions of criticism, to the task of penetrating the deepest realms of motive within the creative impulse of single persons and in whole societies—in Brooks, America had found the critic who established the conditions which enabled high art to flourish. No one else had Brooks's "depth of insight into the nature of American life and of human life in general," Rosenfeld agreed, "the erudition, the sense of the function of art, and the knowledge of psychological theory." Brooks, "you must realize what an inciter to flame in others you are," Sherwood Anderson said. And his opinion was all but unanimous among those younger writers who had chosen not to pursue Pound's course, or Eliot's, had not chosen escape from rather than reform of the life of letters in America. And who were bored or infuriated by the cascades of chitchat—Ernest Boyd in the *Bookman*, Llewellyn Jones in the *Chicago Post*, Francis Hackett, Burton Rascoe—which passed for criticism in America.

A certain restraint of applause was noticeable, however, among those admirers who found Brooks wanting in fidelity of another kind, to that other chief function of criticism which Eliot came to represent, the view which insisted that a critic must give the hardest and closest attention to text and context: formalism. Although no one disputed Brooks's claim to eminence, not everyone shared Mrs. Colum's or Rosenfeld's taste in criticism, or Anderson's excitement. For Gorham Munson's essay convincingly showed—an essay addressed to those of the *Dial*'s readers who preferred Eliot's position—that literary judgment which "wants to be social and genetic" must not neglect the study of those formal properties which give shape to single works. Moral fervor is no substitute for analytic criticism.

It is well known that the beginnings of a major battle of the books occur here, a battle which only now, its main opponents dead, is pretty much exhausted. Although William Carlos Williams along the way replaced Brooks as a leader of the opposition to Eliot, it was Brooks around whom the battle had raged at its moment of origin and who, well into the forties, had retained the allegiance of Eliot's adversaries. By then, however, Brooks had got deep into that series of volumes in literary history which led him to enlarge the debate to include matters more momentous than either literary theory or literary politics. Indeed, a 1939 symposium in the *Partisan Review*, "The Literary Situation in American Writing," reprinted in *The Partisan Reader* (1946), opened its questionnaire with the very problems—about the existence of a usable past, about the relative importance of James and Whitman—which Brooks had made fashionable. Similarly, Stanley Edgar Hyman, writing *The Armed Vision* mainly in tribute to Kenneth Burke, was unable to record his judgment of Burke's importance without accounting for Brooks's. As in the *Partisan Review* and *The Armed Vision*, so in seminar at Columbia: during the late forties I would pass Brooks in the library, would often find his signature on loan cards, would find these trivial things impressive because, going from library to class, I would be expected to exhibit a precise knowledge of Brooks's ideas from *America's Coming-of Age* to *The Flowering of New England* and the *Opinions of Oliver Allston*. But never beyond.

Until the early fifties, therefore, Brooks was a presence. Unfortunately, the 1950s were disastrous for idealogues of Brooks's persuasion. The clairvoyance of Brooks's alter ego, Oliver Allston, was forgotten and only his retrograde opinions were recalled. These were the opinions which supported Brooks's utopism. And utopism of any kind bore no relation either to American domestic policy during the McCarthy years or to cold war politics during the Dulles years. Furthermore, Brooks's urbane eloquence in praise of the pastoral virtues seemed merely to dramatize that nostalgia of general culture and blankness of mind, in the face of desperate problems, which marked the Eisenhower years. Suddenly Brooks's presence vanished—only the legend, now substantially altered, was left. And in 1963 when the man died, there were eulogies by J. Donald Adams and Brooks Atkinson in the *New York Times*, by Malcolm Cowley in the *Saturday Review*. But in the universities, in the literary reviews, scarcely a word: Charles Angoff's essay is, I think, the sole exception.

Grim fate for a former oracle. And it would be grimmer still if current generations of scholars, students, critics—and the Common Reader—were to decide that the legend has some value but the work of sixty years of professional life is barely worth preserving. Fame which rests on personality alone is of low order and seldom survives the memory of the person. The question of Brooks's fame, of Brooks's fate, became a subject of conversation with Delmore Schwartz about a year before Schwartz died, near the end of the spring term when there was time for talk. He asked if I had learned anything which might renew or sustain or reinstate Brooks's reputation. It was a matter of special interest to Schwartz, I knew, because he had been an editor of the *Partisan Review* at the exact moment when, according to William Phillips and Philip Rahv, that journal had undertaken to oppose the "regressive" trend implicit in the "neo-Americanism of Brooks, DeVoto, and a host of lesser patriots." Schwartz had been also one of the brightest of that group of "urban critics" and "stern academic professionals" to whom Daniel Aaron had referred (Hyman, F. W. Dupee, Oscar Cargill) who "resented what they considered [Brooks's] parochialism and his celebration of books and writers and literary tendencies he had once condemned."

No, I had not solved the problem of Brooks. But I was drawn to the argument René Wellek had made in a 1942 essay which, taking up causes then in disfavor, had never got the attention it had warranted. Wellek had taxed Brooks for perpetrating error and cliché and thereby contributing to the decline of literary history. But he had admired the romantic strain in Brooks's thought. Although he agreed

6 THE LEGACY OF VAN WYCK BROOKS

that Brooks's bludgeoning attack on modern writers was
deplorable, nevertheless Wellek found commendable the
"uncommon frankness and boldness" with which Brooks
vented a widespread disaffection with certain debased tendencies in modernist writing. In his "emotional, quite un-
theoretical way Mr. Brooks gives voice to a genuine need of
the time: a return to the sources of the American national
tradition which fortunately is also the hope of all humanity."
Setting aside those "distressingly Darwinistic formulas for
good writing" which Brooks seemed to enjoy inventing,
Wellek preferred to stress the nineteenth-century romantic,
liberal, humanitarian, and visionary temper of Brooks's
mind. For he found Brooks's definition of the role of the
writer in human civilization to accord not only with the
great motifs of the romantic tradition but also to reinforce
some main motifs in American thought. By no means ex-
clusively American these are perhaps best taken Brooks's
way, as American par excellence.

It won't work, Schwartz said. It leaves out the chauvinism
and therefore doesn't account for the central enigma of
Brooks's career: after he had turned his back on the vanguard, he had turned up as a leader of the rearguard, unable
to decide whether he was a patriot of Westport, Connecticut, or a "transnationalist" of cosmopolitan America—a man
merely rural-minded or a man, like his hero H. G. Wells, of
planetary imagination. And because chauvinism followed
the period of emotional breakdown, the problem lay in the
causes and consequences of trauma during that period of
crisis, 1926 to 1930. This was of course a familiar and con-
ventional view and its implications have been stressed by
Sherman Paul: "Brooks is perhaps the last American writer
to feel so intensely the American problem of Europe and
America. It is understandable that the emotional difficulties
of solving this complicated problem contributed to Brooks's
breakdown and to the conception of an organic New England community that flowered out of it."

Brooks, too, long afterward had himself traced his rediscovery of America to those years of self-discovery, but his
own view was so simplistic as to seem flatly incredible. "One

of the doctors whom I saw and who had read *The Ordeal of Mark Twain* asked me if I considered that 'reason' or 'emotion' had been the determining element in my mind and work." "Reason, I suppose." But the doctor smiled, shook his head, walked away. "I saw at once that he was right." Had it really been incidents of this kind which had convinced him that he'd been on the wrong track when it was clear to everyone, even his opponents, that he'd taken a tack which really led somewhere? If breakdown exhibited a failure of conviction, what had therapy achieved? Had treatment taken the wind out of his sails? But what system of therapy could have got him turned round so, could have convinced a man of his extraordinary and subtle mind that the language of praise presents intelligence in its healthy state and the language of condemnation exhibits the mind in a state of disease? Who or what had converted him to the belief that he had been evading his deepest nature during that first period and that he had arrived at the condition of profoundest self-confrontation and self-perception during that second period? For surely he had spoken cogently, reasonably, about the real state of affairs in America during those years when, so he later thought, he had been in a state of malaise. In speaking of ruin Brooks flourished. But when he believed himself to be in the state of deepest accord with the meaning of American experience, he had spun out a marvelous, ingenious, exquisite fantasy—America in homespun—which most reasonable men today admire but reject.

Brooks's own explanation of these shifts in direction ("I conducted my education in public") is far less telling than Oscar Cargill's acute observation, that Brooks's response to critical assault, before 1925, was typical of his career in general: "he visibly yielded ground." During his later life, indeed, he staked out his claim on ground so high that none of his critics could plague him. And after 1940, when he had published the first two volumes in the Makers and Finders series, *The Flowering of New England* and *New England: Indian Summer*, very few of his critics chose to follow let alone to pursue him. Even Malcolm Cowley, a very loyal disciple and old friend, felt compelled to deprecate Brooks's

preference for "historical portraits that seem completely in-
sulated from the life that used to inspire him to hope or
anger." So complete was this insulation that Brooks lost the
public which had formerly cherished his work but, para-
doxically, found himself adored by the very audience he had
formerly attacked: the highbrow critic acquired lowbrow
fame. Then in 1941 with the appearance of *Oliver Allston*,
he burned his bridges. "The literary mind of our time is
sick"—this was his judgment of the main tendencies of a
period which, though bleak, was blessed by a bounty of
genius for which he himself had prepared the way. "If only
that chapter" on coterie-literature had been left out, Allen
Tate is supposed to have said, "how much happier we should
all have been."

Distressed and puzzled by this transformation, this ab-
dication, no one questioned Brooks's motives just his judgment—which his old comrade-at-arms of the *Seven Arts*,
Waldo Frank, called prejudiced and uninformed. In a letter
to Brooks in 1951, Frank confessed that his hurt was personal but his dissent was professional. Reading the last
volume in Makers and Finders, *The Confident Years*, he
asked why Brooks felt compelled to disregard the work of
his closest colleagues, Frank himself, Lewis Mumford, above
all William Carlos Williams, whose support of the utopist
tradition in American letters was at least as persistent and
profound as Brooks's own. Here was a grave flaw, Frank said,
fatal in a writer of Brooks's kind. For the critic whose paramount passion is the morality of art cannot afford, either
out of ignorance or some schizoid ceremoniousness to disregard those writers whose thought has expressed his own
values. For all his merit, he cannot retain the respect of
those to whom his attack on false values must in the end
seem inauthentic and invalid.

By the early fifties, then, when Brooks's ideology was itself undermined by events, he had lost the confidence of
even his own former allies. Instead, according to Glenway
Wescott's eulogy, he had become once again a figure of
legend, incarnation of the heroic life in art. The man whose
romantic cast of mind had led him into cul-de-sac became

himself a figure of romance. Unlike a wide group of twenties writers, among whom Leslie Fiedler recently placed John Peale Bishop, who refused to accommodate themselves to a new era and a new politics but continued to subscribe to the "religion of art," to express a "righteous contempt for the vulgarities of American culture," and to yearn for "the Old World Charm"—unlike Bishop and others who fled to Europe, Brooks stayed. From the mid-thirties to the early sixties he had read thousands of books, had composed by hand many thousands of pages of manuscript. Heroic indeed, said the obituary editorial in the *New York Times*, worth accolade of the rarest kind, the life and achievement of this exemplary American scholar. A recipient of honorary degrees from Columbia, Bowdoin, Tufts, Dartmouth, Union, Northwestern, and other less impressive places, of countless other honors, a leading figure at the American Academy of Arts and Letters, Fellow of the Royal Society of Literature, Brooks—said the *Times*—must be ranked with the tiny handful of great critics, Poe and Eliot and Edmund Wilson, developed in the United States.

Leaving out details and skimping touchy subjects, I responded to Schwartz's inquiry. I talked fast but he, no patient listener, hummed sounds and smoked handfuls of cigarettes. "But it's so simple, the solution," he said. "They brainwashed him. In those hospitals. That's why I won't have anything to do with them, psychiatrists, psychoanalysts. They ruin you. Not Freud but the others, the epigones, they iron you out and there's nothing left but to fold." Till that moment our talk had been easy but Schwartz, when I knew him in the early sixties, sat under the volcano of his vices and it was impossible to anticipate the instant when an explosion was due. "It's a terrible thing they did to him. All the wildness and intensity of his first work, the *Coming-of-Age*, that messily Freudian but really marvelous book on Mark Twain—the James was just bad—really mattered to people. I mean he was read, argued through, believed in and fought over, passionately. Me too. I reviewed one of his books, *New England: Indian Summer*, I think, and he wrote me a note and we corresponded but by then he was a spook."

Schwartz's own distinguishing trait as a writer, in verse and prose, had been a matter of flowing cadences and hard edges, of faith in the measure and power of reason even in our age of unreason.

> Once, when I was a boy
> Apollo summoned me
> To be apprenticed to an endless summer of light
>   and consciousness
> And thus to become and be what poets often have
>   been.

But he had not managed to fulfill that enormous expectation of career which this sort of work, "Once and for All," had roused. By 1964, measure and power were gone and instead there was an access of cunning as well as excess of every kind: thought, talk, drink, smoke, love, hate. "I don't know why, just because you've been in a nuthouse people think— nobody will listen even if you speak the truth. Psychotic." He was talking to an audience, suddenly, which both included and excluded me and I couldn't interrupt. "Unless you've been psychoanalyzed. Then it's glorious, then it's even better than simply being normal, a sign of grace. But suppose psychosis clarifies things? Poe. And you know Brooks never had the least idea what Poe was all about. But that was later—up to 1920 or so Brooks really understood what was going on, told about it, tried to suffer through the pain of his vision until they made a sane man of him. Right this minute I know what's going on too, down in Albany, and that's why they mean to make me sane too and that kind of sanity you can ———." He caught himself, stopped, left. I was gone for a year and in the interim he died.

What survives that hour's talk, survives even the madness of its last minute, is a matter of *déjà vu*: as Brooks's life, committed to the Apollonian idea, in the end seemed to parody Schwartz's art, so Schwartz's life turned out to be a surreal imitation of Brooks's thought. For here was still another remarkably vivid and poignant instance of the blighted life in American letters against which Brooks had railed during those first flaming years of prophecy. Ironically, too, Schwartz's judgment of Brooks, translated from the language of psychopathology, virtually duplicates Brooks's famed opinion on the causes of Mark Twain's failure, Mark Twain's despair. Within every man, Brooks had said in 1920, citing Sainte-Beuve, there is a poet who dies young. And this malady, this miscarriage of the inner life, is epidemic in the United States where an "unconscious conspiracy" generated by "capitalistic industrialism" imprisons the free spirit, the creative spirit. So profoundly engrained in our consciousness is this notion that now, its origins lost, it is taken as axiomatic truth. An ulcer, gentlemen, John Ciardi not very long ago told a group of dispirited businessmen who sought liberation by way of literature—an ulcer is an unwritten poem.

The first half of Brooks's polemical career was spent in demonstrating the ulcerous effects of America on the human spirit: Delmore Schwartz. And the second half of his career was spent in effort to prove that the very word *America*, in its root meaning, signified the spirit of health: Helen Keller. Was ever the physical life of man or woman more radically disfigured than Miss Keller's? Was ever the contour and lineament of moral health given more vivid configuration? "I thought of Helen when I read" in Arthur Koestler's *The Age of Longing* that American women were too busy playing bridge to be cut out for the part of martyrs and saints. Clearly Koestler had missed the point of America, had not got the point of James's *The Portrait of a Lady*, of Isabel Archer whom Helen Keller resembled in her "fixed determination to regard the world as a place of brightness, of free expansion, of irresistible action." Miss Keller's decision, that "life was worth living only if one moved in the realm of light," thus represented a personal victory and a national conquest, triumph of American vitality and buoyancy. Didact to the end, Brooks was convinced that the spirit's health was confirmed by those powers of "affirmative vision" inherent within the unconscious American "collective literary mind" which, as revealed in Makers and Finders, enables us to revere, promote, maintain, renew our "dream of utopia." And although he realized, two years before his death, that he was known mainly as the author of *America's Coming-of-Age* and *The Ordeal of Mark Twain*—most critics felt that "the rest was best not mentioned"—he confessed that his "chief hope for some kind of relative permanence was in my historical series."

Because these questions implicate issues which are irremediably complex, I have hoped to crystallize the whole matter by way of a drama of character, Brooks and Schwartz, Brooks and Helen Keller. Can the case of Schwartz be said to represent the persistence and power of Brooks's first intuitions? Probably yes. But can the example of Helen Keller, a sport of history, be taken to represent the triumph of America, of light over darkness, of eros over thanatos—of Brooks and Mumford over Eliot and Pound? Probably not. *Makers and Finders* is no masterpiece, in my view, and its ideology has been in some small degree baneful. For it has been a main source of inspiration of one of the most influential textbooks in our time, Robert Spiller's *Literary History of the United States*. In most respects this is a splendid synthesis of ideas, men and movements in the American past, but its thesis (a "happy and forward-looking literature has been produced by a happy and forward-looking people," one critic said) has imposed a "tendentiousness on American literature that it does not, except in small part, actually have." Not until the publication of another tendentious work of literary history, Fiedler's *Love and Death in the American Novel*, which stressed the Gothic mode, gloom and ruin and terror, did that other radical theme of Brooks's critical imagination acquire the scale and weight it deserved.

Makers and Finders, then, is less a masterpiece than it is a monument. And its five volumes offer matter for a dozen additional books not on the vast themes to which the *Literary History* and *Love and Death* are devoted but on the biographies of single persons who came to life in Brooks's pages. These figures are of no great moment in the American past; none is in any deep sense "usable." But most are vital for a recreation of the density and variety of life in that sparsely settled land: Lorenzo da Ponte, Mozart's librettist in Vienna, converted Jew, abbé, friend of Casanova in Venice, turns up a grocer in Sunbury, Pennsylvania, during the early 1800s and later appears, a teacher of Italian, in New York, where in 1825 *Don Giovanni* had its first American performance. More than antiquarian taste is roused by the idea of this man in Sunbury.

Brooks's "stringent demands for a culture adequate to our needs were the strongest influence on my own first work," F. O. Matthiessen said in *American Renaissance* (1941). Matthiessen's tribute is not just a confession of personal bent. It is rather, as younger critics do not recognize, an accurate appraisal of Brooks's influence on the general reader, on two generations of literary reformers and intellectuals in America. What a paradox it is to discover, even among Matthiessen's admirers, a pervasive ignorance of Brooks's example—not Irving Babbitt's or Paul Elmer More's or H. L. Mencken's or that of any other figure in our recent past—as a source of inspiration, avatar of the literary life in America. I mention these particular names, incidentally, because this group along with Matthiessen appear in a new book, Richard Ruland's *The Rediscovery of American Literature* (1968), treating the period 1900 to 1940. Because it is Matthiessen on whom the weight of attention falls, it is inexcusable that a book which bears this title should merely skim the surfaces of Brooks's thought. For even if we set aside all considerations of precise influence, the bald fact is that even so recently as 1948, H. W. Wilson and Company, publishers of reference works, tabulations, indices of one kind or another, described Brooks as the most widely read author of the decade which ended in 1945. And even if Mr. Ruland—I concentrate fire here only because the target's there—should find Brooks unimposing, still he might have been guided by F. R. Leavis's judgment, in a 1952 essay called "The Americanness of American Literature." Whatever may be Brooks's "distinctive mark in the contemporary American literary world, the five-volume work that comes to a close with *The Confident Years* seems to me to be in an essential respect very representative— representative, I mean, of a prevailing climate."

My account of Brooks's legacy takes Matthiessen's tribute as a point of genesis and Leavis's appraisal as a point of terminus. And because once again the Young Generation, as fifty years ago Brooks described himself and his peers, struggles to create a culture adequate to its needs, perhaps the time is right to rediscover the reasons why this modest, resolute, gentle and heroic man came to serve as the representative genius of American letters during the first age of transformation in our time.

2

From Frying Pan to Fire

> He has always been drawn away from the literary document
> in front of him to a portrait of its author, or a diagnosis of
> his or his character's or his nation's psychology, or a disserta-
> tion on a state of society, or the recreation of a former epoch,
> or a programme for American culture.—Gorham B. Munson,
> 1925

In 1925, having published eight studies in literary criticism
and history, in polemic and biography, Brooks was generally
regarded as the undisputed heir of and spokesman for the
great tradition in American thought—the radical, reformist,
prophetic, organic tradition which adopted Emerson as its
source of inspiration, *The American Scholar* as its point of
departure, and envisioned as its point of terminus the creation of a civilization in which the creative spirit, in all its
social and imaginative forms, might flourish. To this old
enterprise Brooks had brought a cosmopolitan experience,
a well-stocked mind, intransigent zeal, incomparable flair—
a genius for clarifying thought, said his colleague of the
Seven Arts, James Oppenheim. To the presumably definitive
study of this tradition in classic and contemporary American
letters, Richard Poirier in *A World Elsewhere* (1966) has
brought considerable flair and too a disdain, both symptomatic and wanton, for Brooks's sovereign role.

"The most interesting American books," Poirier observes,
"are an image of the creation of America itself, of the effort,
in the words of Emerson's Orphic poet, to 'Build therefore

your own world.' " A half century ago exactly this kind of exhortation underlay the decision of certain young men to go to London and Paris: only outside the United States, in the great European capitals, could American genius flourish. Brooks, who at first shared their view, eventually came to think that America, by virtue of its history and ideology, was not only itself the very emblem of the creative life but was, too, the best place on earth to locate the republic of letters. And he composed a series of books which monumentalized Emerson's Orphic vision. Suddenly, when his art had achieved certain marvels of transformation, he lost voice, heart, taste, courage for the task. Somehow he lost the thread of his own passion and found himself in an abyss of his own devising. A really major figure in the seedtime of modern thought, he became a minor figure in the time of efflorescence—victim of the very forces he had discerned, named, and condemned.

There was no external sign of faltering will in those early books, written at white heat between 1908 and 1925, which introduced a prodigy endowed with audacity of learning, fluency of speech, an apparent assurance of mind, and a cosmopolitan experience unmatched in American criticism of that day. Born in Plainfield, New Jersey, in 1886, educated there and in Europe where his family had spent a year in 1898, Brooks had entered Harvard in 1904. Completing his degree a year early, in 1907, he had come to New York as a free lance of letters. His mind full of ideas for books, impatient for fortune enough to marry Eleanor Kenyon Stimson, whom he had known as a friend of childhood and youth, hot for fame, he had gone on a third European journey, to England, where for a year and a half he had lived as he could and where he had written and published—subsidizing half the cost—*The Wine of the Puritans* in 1908. Back in New York that year, aged twenty-two, well-placed to advance his career, he had remained until 1911, still on Grub Street, working on the *Standard Dictionary, Collier's Encyclopedia,* laboring as an editorial assistant on the *World's Work.* "Well, I saw Mr. William Dean Howells, who . . . is most agreeable and charming,"

he had written to his fiancée in 1907. "He said that he knew
very little about journalism, but was ever so nice and genial,
and made up in good feeling for what he lacked in advice.
But such a funny little round-shouldered *bunch* of a man!—
He almost rolled about the floor rather than walked, and
his kind face was like crepe for wrinkles! Darling, if this
description is unkind, it shows a lack of genius in me, for I
would give a great deal for the proper words to tell how
cordial and good-humoured and sympathetic he was. Then
I went to see Mr. Paul E. More, the editor of the Evening
Post and the Nation. . . . He seemed a little indefinite
about what I must do, but he gave me a very interesting
book of miscellaneous essays . . . to write a short review of
for the Nation, which he said he might or might not use.
But the day after I had sent him my review, the proof came
back, and so I suppose it will appear this week; but it is not
of the slightest account, dear, because it only takes up about
three inches in a single column, and is in all ways quite
ordinary. They say that I must write articles on contemporary
writers and send them about to the newspapers, and this is
the way to begin—which I shall do at once. . . . It seems
to me so infinitely important, this *getting somewhere* . . .
but this living-by-your-wits! You may strike a gold-mine, you
may suddenly wake up famous,—or—you may go hungry for
months."

In his autobiography he speaks briefly and lightly of this
period, of "marking time in these miscellaneous drudgeries
of the literary tyro," time relieved by listening to the talk
of John Butler Yeats, the poet's father, at Petitpas, a board-
ing house and restaurant frequented by the Ashcan painters,
Robert Henri, John Sloan, Glackens, Prendergast. And indeed at first his tone had been light, the excitement of doing
the world's work among some of its leading figures being
enough to carry him through. The expectation of reward
had been the ground of hope: Brooks had vowed to get on
fast. But from the beginning he had been a displaced person
in New York. "I look forward almost with horror to the day,"
he wrote Miss Stimson in 1909, "to the thunder of the
trains, to the awkward haste of city crowds, to the evil heat

of the subways, the crashing & rushing of the midsummer city. . . . I am also realizing how deep is my dislike toward the office, in which none of my normal functions are in play. Is it narrow or cowardly? I think not. Behind work there must exist first *order*, then *hope*: and it is right that we should give out what we contain—if we contain anything. Of late I have almost forgotten a certain peace of mind & forbearance which enabled me to keep a sort of superior feeling—superior only for self-preservation. . . . I have been living & talking with people in New York who do not recognize the existence of a life devoted to art, which does not possess the tangible signs of a paintbox or a violin. These people tell me that art is only a branch of life, that art is becoming a branch of sociology, etc. They do not hesitate to prattle about art without first thinking that art demands a special, an intense devotion. And they expect those who think about art to think also about the cotton crop, as if we were already living in that beautiful golden age when everybody will know so much about everything that a poet and a crossing-sweeper (or rather a 'captain of industry') will exchange functions without losing identity. . . . Art is born of confusion, waste, prodigality, error, lost causes. . . . I hate and distrust the trend of things. We do not stagnate if we react violently enough! . . . I hate the whole race—and especially their superficial optimism, the result of large dividends. You cannot conceive how commercial the very fabric of this nation is." Brooks concludes his tirade on themes he was to sort out before long in *America's Coming-of-Age.**

* From the very first, his love of Europe was suffused by his pathological distaste for the whole American business of money. A letter written to Eleanor Stimson from Naples in 1905 most cogently concentrates these radical traits of Brooks's temper: "What a place Naples is! . . . No fevered imagination could picture anything worse. And yet what a pity it is that a Hell for Humanity is so often a Paradise for Artists. They are so beautifully miserable! The beggars covered in patches, the children wholly naked, all diseased, weary, mis-shapen. What far better pictures they make than Bank Presidents or American grocers." Although Brooks was a boy when these lines were set down, his mind continued to play with permutations of meaning conceived on this second European visit.

By January 1911, Brooks could neither bear New York nor the distance separating him from Berkeley, where Miss Stimson lived. "I had not thoroughly learned the relation between myself & New York. My position here is no longer feasible—of that I am certain. Each month I feel more full of self-confidence, more certain of real growth, real intellectual development in myself. And as I seem to take form I revolt more and more from the kind of work I am doing. It is shabby, dishonest work, indeed. . . . The whole literary situation is not fit to bring oneself into contact with. . . . I have written to Dean Briggs in Cambridge to pull the wires at Leland Stanford. . . . I really do count on this. I count so entirely that I plan to go West in another six weeks in any case! I have, suddenly, all the feelings of a successful man! . . . I am going to be very important. I am going to present myself with a very bold face, tell everybody that I am a brilliant young scholar." And so he was, and so he went. And for all his lamentations—chiefly centered on the delay of marriage, the cost of poverty, the evasiveness of fame—Brooks started early, came on strong, and lasted long.

At Carmel later that year he married Eleanor Stimson whose own life, before and after Wellesley college, had been spent going back and forth from Europe: "We were both in love with Europe and always had been." Consequently, their stay in California was short and in 1913 they returned to England—a son had been born in 1912—where he published the work done during the quick western years, *The Malady of the Ideal*. This and *The Wine of the Puritans* make a pair quite as the next two, *John Addington Symonds: A Biography* (1914) and *The World of H. G. Wells* (1914), were conceived and composed in concert. All four, taken together, represent initial statements of those ideas, passionately held, which were to shape Brooks's critique of and program for America in the celebrated essays *America's Coming-of-Age* (1915), *Letters and Leadership* (1918), and the psychological studies, *The Ordeal of Mark Twain* (1920), and *The Pilgrimage of Henry James* (1925). In these eight interconnected pieces of work, representing nearly two decades of resolute and concentrated labor, Brooks focussed his whole energy on a single theme. He sought to penetrate the conditions which devastate and to disclose the environments which nurture the springs of art in Europe and the United States.

I speak of these intricate things as if there is no problem in reducing a thousand pages of intense prose—and hundreds of pages of criticism of Brooks's prose—to a simple formula. But the very resourcefulness of Brooks's mind and the opulence of comment on Brooks's books have obscured certain obvious matters about which it is, at this late-stage judgment, no great task to be forthright. Indeed, a certain likeness from book to book has always been fairly plain. Stanley Edgar Hyman, for example, describing Brooks's distinction between the actual "wine" of the Puritans and the "aroma" of wine, recognized in this play of metaphor an embryonic version of those distinctions between highbrow and lowbrow on which Brooks was to build the myth of America's coming of age. If you read backwards from lowbrow you discover Brooks maintaining that it was the Puritans' taste for the material life of the New World which led in later centuries to a sheer and bald commercialism: "wine." Read backwards from highbrow and you find Brooks arguing that it was the Puritans' simultaneous joy in the "aroma of the wine, the emphasis on the ideal, which became transcendentalism." The essential questions raised in *The Wine of the Puritans*, then, introduced a perplexity which was ever to vex Brooks, a man who retained all his life the habit of formulating modern questions in an archaic language. If art is defined as the soul's perception of the ideal, how can art enrich a society which was itself created out of a breach between soul and body, between ideal and real? Could America be made into a place where the life of thought and the life of action might be reconciled? Was Brooks himself equipped to undertake the hard work of reconciliation? Did high art have a chance in the United States?

In these reflections there is an echo of an aesthete's bull session over fin de siècle sherry in the Yard at Harvard— perhaps with John Hall Wheelock, the undergraduate friend with whom Brooks collaborated in a volume of verse, privately printed in 1905; or with Edward Sheldon, to whom Brooks dedicated *The Malady of the Ideal,* or most certainly with his boyhood friend of Plainfield, New Jersey, Maxwell Perkins, to whom the book on Symonds was dedicated. Perkins, later a distinguished editor, was to serve as godfather to Fitzgerald and Hemingway and Thomas Wolfe, to hosts of writers and books in our era. Whether or not he became Brooks's mentor too is unclear. But during these years the two men talked and corresponded, conducted a continuing conversation on precisely the issues which Brooks sought to unravel in his first books. A letter from Perkins to Brooks (May 20, 1915, written from a hospital bed in which Perkins was recovering from an operation which he described as having been so simple as to call for no comment) returns to the subject they had discussed last spring: America can be considered a place of hope and promise because it stands on the verge of radical change. Instead of an economic life guided by competition, we face an era in which the production of necessities would be so apportioned among men that an almost negligible part of man's time would be given to this purely material work. Human energy, freed from what Perkins called animal demands, might be turned toward spiritual channels. For isn't it true that Americans now hold all the arts in contempt because love of them curbs a man in competition? If we banish competition and abolish slavery, don't we free Americans from sloth and dissipation? Can't we then free the life of the spirit?

The preoccupations of Brooks's published writing mirrored this exchange of views whether or not the books included that particular set of ideas—quite as the correspondence with Miss Stimson, a few years earlier, permitted Brooks to explain to himself his purposes in *The Wine of the Puritans.* In Capri during 1908, when he was in England, she received his manuscript and a detailed account of points made on a subject to which each was devoted, qualities and contrasts of America and Europe. "I say that it is because of this 'brooding melancholy' that Europe is what it is: or rather I say that the grace, the ease, the polish, the charm, the traditional ingrained mellowness of the upper classes of Europe are the *converse* of this pessimism, that the splendor of the enlightened is the result of the sorrows of the peasantry, and that that splendor and those sorrows are bound together by a brooding melancholy which constitutes the ancient and profound sadness of European history and politics and religion and art—in a word of European society. That is the note, in the last analysis, of Ibsen & Maeterlinck, Hauptmann & D'Annunzio,—Scandinavia, France (Belgium), Germany & Italy. It is the note of a sorrowful protest that life is what it is. . . . I too allowed myself that note. . . . Alas! Dear me, it is so hard for me to reconcile myself to the inexorable belief that we must wait through long centuries of harsh untutored endeavour in our dear country before we too can have that mellowed splendor: yes, and that when that splendor comes it will come as the converse of melancholy and decay. I do feel that the crudeness of our American temper strikes the note of a rationalism which will sweep away these ashes over which the heart lingers with such poignant regret. . . . There is no place in this system for any sadness except the sadness of personal bereavement and personal failure. But there is in the human heart a yearning and a racial melancholy, a desire for unnamed things greater than any personal issues and which the human heart does not want to understand. . . . I see that you have given me much food for thought, and I think now that if my book comes back from the publisher I shall reconstruct it and add to it, for I think now that I was ill-advised in writing so hastily and that I see the possibility of a greater synthesis. . . ."

This letter is rather more solemn and elevated than most. But it does indeed very accurately display the sort of conversation not uncommon among the highest minded men and women of Brooks's day—even as it discloses Brooks's passion for those great designs and lofty fables of the soul which generated his first books. Invariably cast into pairs of metaphor, these matters represent the main pursuits of Brooks's imagination from first to last. In *The Malady of the Ideal*, for example, his passion for syntheses of this sort is expressed in a contrast of the nature and temper of German thought with the French. The French temperament, fixed firmly in the real world and engaged by the problems of social order, he called *rhetorical*. In contrast, the German mind, concerned with "truth, good, and beauty," the realm of the ideal, was *poetical* in its drift. In Brooks's own mind, the charm of these distinctions lay in their utility as definitions of the nature of poetry and the nature of rhetoric. The true poet, rooted in the real, fixed his attention unwaveringly on the ideal and became therefore a great source of reconciliation, a visionary of order on earth. A rhetorician, however, was committed to the study of exterior consistency alone. "He takes his point of departure from an idea which in its primitive form is a sincere expression of himself. The next day looking deeper he perhaps discovers a new idea that cuts away the ground from under his former idea. But he is a practical man—he . . . therefore forces a consistency between the two ideas." As the circle of his thought arcs farther and farther away from that first, genuine perception, finally "he achieves a logical consistency; his work has a compact, finished quality. But where is truth?" Illustrating the practical effects of his theory, Brooks referred to Senancour, Maurice de Guérin, and arrived at last at Amiel, "true child of Geneva," in whom French and German influence came to stand-off, a sterile, immobilizing "fatal mixture of the blood." Neither German enough, "foolhardy" enough, to trust an intuition, nor French enough, rhetorical enough, to rely on disciplined rationalism, Amiel sat "like a spider in a kind of comic web spun from his own body, unable to find himself because he could not lose himself."

Before long, as we shall see, Brooks himself was to arrive at the condition in which *The Malady of the Ideal* leaves Amiel. Unfortunately, too, his next books, on Symonds and Wells, mark the emergence of Brooks the rhetorician, the practical critic whose work was compact and self-contained and consistent but—said his critics—Where was truth? It was a question which was to plague him throughout his life. In spite of vow and disavowal, the rhetorician's habit of work was one he simply could not resist. "I was obliged to force individuals into general categories, to fit complex persons into beds of Procrustes," he confessed much later in autobiography. In the book on Symonds he took his point of departure from an idea which, inadvertently, was more a "sincere expression of himself" than a judgment of Symonds. And in the book on Wells he set out a thesis so procrustean that, as Oscar Cargill remarked, the critics flayed him alive.

Writing a rhetorician's book on Symonds, Brooks made a safari through the thicket of his subject's unconscious. Ordinarily this little book is dismissed. Even Paul Rosenfeld, accustomed to weigh everything, in 1925 wrote the first full appraisal of Brooks's thought and said merely that Brooks remained well outside Symonds. A disappointing book to read in 1914, it is an especially rewarding book to read now. For Brooks was only superficially preoccupied with his ostensible subject and was deeply engaged inquiring into his essential subject—himself. In its tiniest detail and in the sweep of its theme, the biography of Symonds is a clairvoyant essay in self-appraisal and self-revelation.

Taking up the subject of his *Malady*, applying its theoretical system to English letters, Brooks presents Symonds as a victim of neuroticism so acute as render him blind to the distinction between "mundane and visionary values," between real and ideal. Unlike Amiel, Symonds found himself mired not in mere impasse but in the state of total dysfunction. Incapable of sustaining that "prolonged and chronic tension which brought the malady of Amiel"—that thirst for the absolute—"to such exquisite heights," unable to sustain infinite tension, Symonds was quick to accept a "makeshift." Makeshift was one of Brooks's key words of the moment and was intended to connote that combination of ideas which in philosophic thought does not love metaphysics. Anything that represents an effort to perceive mere "order in the world has been a makeshift," Brooks had said in the *Malady*.

Symonds to his credit possessed a visionary mind; to his discredit, so Brooks believed, he was incapable of bearing the cost of vision and he turned instead to rhetoric, to the study of the humdrum. In order to support this reading, Brooks adopted a strategy which led him away from the ordinary pursuits of literary criticism and plunged him into the first of his exercises in the psychology of failure, the sociology of despair. Whatever else must be said, it cannot be gainsaid that this was pioneer work of a most taxing kind. And what has hitherto been left unsaid about Brooks is that his pioneering studies in literary psychology were informed by his reading in a single source, Bernard Hart's *The Psychology of Insanity*. This famous handbook was first published in England in 1912, shortly before Brooks's second English sojourn in 1913, when he returned to Britain for a stay of eighteen months in order to teach in the Worker's Educational Association. As he later told Robert Spiller, Hart's little book represented all that he knew of psychoanalysis.* Whether or not he read Freud or Jung too, whom he mentions in print now and then, is uncertain. But there is no mention of Hart's work in Brooks's writing—a strange omission in the light of his remark to Spiller. Stranger still, indeed, this excision of detail from Brooks's autobiography, for that book is more a meticulous record of the transactions of his mind than it is an account of his life.

The Psychology of Insanity is a historic work. It is the first essay, both technical and lucid, which incorporates Freud's views on the general subject. This book, Hart wrote, "does not really occupy any definite place in the direct line of Freudian history, but is at once narrower and wider in its aim." It is narrower in that it deals with certain selected aspects of Freud's thought (Hart adopted the unconscious and the concept of repression but rejected Freud' views on sex) and it is wider "in that it attempts to bring those aspects into relation with lines of advance followed by other investigators." In its own right a remarkably sage and balanced essay, it is typical of its period, too, in its tone of wonder and certainty—wonder that some classic riddles of the psyche had been solved at last, certainty that some

---

* In a letter (October 22, 1968), Mr. Charles Van Wyck Brooks writes: "I can . . . confirm the story about the *Psychology of Insanity*. He impulsively confided it to me once on a walk and never mentioned it again." His father, Mr. Brooks adds, "was personally of an extreme secretiveness with my brother and me."

tentative propositions would turn out dogmatic truth. Although Hart apologized for a tendency to pontificate, warned his readers against dogma, he was himself enthralled by the new tool and the new tongue. Describing a "causal complex," Hart spoke of a man who, complaining that some church bells were disagreeable, became exceedingly upset. His friend was astonished because the bells were famous. Questioning him, the friend learned that "not only were the bells unpleasant but the clergyman in charge of the church wrote extremely bad poetry" and that the clergyman's poetry had been favorably reviewed whereas the other man's poetry had been dispraised. Obviously, Hart said, this situation represented a causal and rivalry complex.

In Hart's habit of discovering simple trauma behind complicated events, Brooks found sanction to support his own custom of searching out a "causal complex" which would simply explain everything. As applied to Symonds, this habit led Brooks to ascribe neurotic failure to a state of war between reason and action, passion and thought. Symonds's thought could not satisfy appetites generated by Symonds's passions; nor could Symonds, for reasons of health and "conscience," translate thought into action. "In those really penetrating sentences" (which Brooks took over from an earlier biographer) "we have the whole story of Symonds"; "it was this complex [which] remained with him to the last" and ended ultimately in breakdown. Upon recovery, he discovered Whitman and through Whitman acquired "a lusty contempt for purely intellectual processes." Recovery of health did not end the war between reason and passion. Instead Symonds struck a bad bargain with his instincts, Brooks said, and in consequence was transformed into a "congested poet" and *vulgariseur*, whose seven-volume *Renaissance in Italy* struggled to do what "only poetry can do" and is therefore best described as "high fantasy" not high accomplishment in humane letters.

Reading this comment on Symonds, anyone with even the skimpiest knowledge of Brooks's career must recognize in the pattern Brooks ascribes to Symonds's life the very pattern which best describes Brooks's life—including the rediscovery of Whitman. If I seem to be forcing a consistency where there is resemblance alone, Brooks's peroration dispels all doubt. The portrait of Symonds, chronology altered but otherwise changed only to include metaphoric rather than literal detail, could stand as a self-portrait: "Neurotic from birth, suppressed and misdirected in education, turned by early environment and by natural affinity into certain intellectual and spiritual channels, pressed into speculation by dogmatic surroundings and aesthetic study, his naturally febrile constitution shattered by over-stimulation, by wanting vitality denied robust creation, by disease made a wanderer, by disease and wandering together aroused to an unending, fretful activity—the inner history of Symonds could be detailed and charted scientifically."

Completing this book and publishing it, in 1913–14, along with *The Malady of the Ideal* and *The World of H. G. Wells*, Brooks returned to America from his third stay abroad. Return itself signified an end to wandering, an end to the disease of indecision which had plagued him since 1907 when he graduated from Harvard. Brooks's wanderings during this period of his life are not just of documentary interest. Nor do these represent more sprightliness of curiosity in a provincial bright young man. It is a rather more radical thing. For it was during these half-dozen years of energetic literary labor, of inquiry into and contrast of certain American and European styles of life, that Brooks cast about—indeed thrashed about—for reasons why he should remain at home or return abroad to live in determined rather than tentative exile. Composing these early works he sought to resolve a disquietude more pressing than troubled Amiel, say, or Symonds. It is useful, therefore, to present a detailed chart of the inner history of Brooks's mind at the moment when he achieved his greatest fame and widest influence.

A "wanderer, the child of some nation yet unborn, smitten with an inappeasable nostalgia for the Beloved Community on the far side of socialism, he carried with him the intoxicating air of that community, the mysterious aroma of its works and ways." These are Brooks's words, written in eulogy to his beloved friend, Randolph Bourne. But again biography and autobiography fuse: the sketch of Bourne is also a work of self-portraiture which intimates the state of Brooks's mind in the period beginning in 1914. Completing the book on Wells, whom he called an "artist of society," Brooks convinced himself that America was ripe for rebirth on the far side of socialism. He convinced himself, too, that Wells was best regarded as the Matthew Arnold of his day because Wells proved that "socialism is itself a natural outgrowth of 'those best things that have been thought and said in the world.'" Brooks's critics tore this notion to shreds because, heartlessly, they took his idea at face value. Perhaps they would have been gentler if they had recognized the con- sistency of Brooks's rhetoric: smitten with an inappeasable nostalgia for utopia, he had convinced himself that a socialist America would be the place in which the life of the mind (the realm of the ideal) and the life of action (the real) might be brought to equilibrium. America, said Brooks, was H. G. Wells "writ large."

The critics might have been gentler, too, had they guessed that Brooks was by no means a man of composed mind but was instead a man of divided will, that the chief obsession of his divided mind was Europe. This obsession he shared, strangely, with the man he most despised, T. S. Eliot. To say that Brooks despised Eliot is no exaggeration. Although his published comment is restrained, his private comment, particularly in the later days of fascism, exhibits a barely controlled revulsion. The "Elioteers" are almost as bad as the Germans, he blurts in a letter (November 1941), to Bliss Perry. The earth isn't big enough to support them alongside decent men, but because they prefer to live in a concentration camp, nobody will have to put them there. Uncharacteristic language but familiar tone: his rancor ran deep. Brooks the diplomatist of literary politics only occa- sionally permitted the polemicist to surface and vent what John Hall Wheelock has described as a faculty for "extraor- dinary vehemence of thought and feeling." Concerning Eliot, Brooks was peculiarly fierce not just because he despised Eliot's ideas but because, deep down, he shared Eliot's taste for the well-upholstered life of a European man of letters.

For all the vehemence of Brooks's rancor, the truth is that both he and Eliot had early been animated by virtually indistinguishable motives. Although their literary programs were largely dissimilar, each was exercised by compelling ambition to acquire intellectual, social, and moral authority in the life of their age. Both young men modelled their lives according to examples given by the New England Brahminical tradition. Both men invented parallel geneologies. And although Eliot's commitment to Europe is the better publicized, along with his determination to make his mark there where literary prestige really mattered, where audiences of the most discriminating kind conferred or withheld honor— nevertheless, as Brooks said in memoir, it had been in the air he and his friends breathed "in college or in home, that one should not 'write for the provinces' but should go to London, in order to begin one's career at the 'centre,' perhaps, 'get in' and get to be known and discussed by the world that counted there."

In Brooks's instance and Eliot's, in Pound's and Conrad Aiken's, John Gould Fletcher's and H. D.'s—that tidal wave of expatriate American writers—the dream of literature was inextricable from the dream of Europe. "In the world I knew" as a child, that well-heeled and well-placed society of the eastern seaboard, Henry Adams's world, "a voyage to Europe was the panacea for every known illness and discontent." Was it merely a child's idea, Brooks wondered, or did not Americans in general imagine that Europe was a "realm of magic, permanently fixed, secure and solid as the Alps . . . inviolate . . . a paradise of culture that had scarcely known a beginning and would never know an end," the one continent "every corner of which stirred in their breasts an emotion evoked by some novelist or artist, some composer or poet." That it was both a proper child's idea and a general idea held in common among cultivated Americans Brooks knew. He knew too that there were two classic ways to resolve the tension of longing. Choose one place or the other; or, despite strain, preserve connection with both. Unlike his compatriots who had few second thoughts about cloaking themselves in the "iridescent fabric" of Europe, unlike others who sought to sustain tension, Brooks was deeply torn.

The causes of conflict lay in the special circumstances of

his early life, that family life which was at once in harmony
and in conflict with the Harvard cult of Europe, incarnate in
Santayana. Why was I abroad, he had forced himself to think
in 1908, in the Sussex farmhouse where he wrote his first
book. "Why was I abroad when I believed in living at home?"
Part of the answer was by no means complicated—though
it did involve some complications within his family. He was
determined to escape Plainfield, New Jersey, and to avoid
the "sadness and wreckage" which diminished the lives of his
father and brother. In that town where Brooks's neighbors
were the "quiet solid men of money, unobtrusive often to
the point of being mousy, whose dwellings lined the streets
of our corner of the town," he had never been at home. Nor
had his brother, Ames, who had solved the problem of
displacement by locating himself as far as possible from
Plainfield: "He walked in front of the early commuters's
train one morning at the Plainfield station." Nor indeed
had Brooks's father—a man of business, doomed to invalid-
ism, yearning for Europe—ever been at home in that suburb
of Wall Street. "Had my father's practical failure in life
over-affected my own mind, as his European associations
had affected it also, so that perhaps his inability to adjust
himself to existence at home had started my own European-
American conflict?"

Although Brooks's thought tends often to lunge toward
the pat answer, he did come to adulthood within a family
in which Europe was represented as the solution for everything. But if his family proved anything it proved that
Europe solved nothing. Eventually, believing that "deracination meant ruin," Brooks found himself impaled: "the
American writer could neither stay *nor* go,—he had only two
alternatives, the frying-pan and the fire." This truly intracta-
ble dilemma it is hard today to recreate. Yet it played a
decisive role in the lives of all those sad young men of good
breeding—Eliot and Edmund Wilson and Brooks are perhaps the most famous—out of Harvard and Princeton and
Columbia, monied, not rich, whose pride of caste lay not
in the accumulation of wealth but in a synthesis of leisure
and labor developed during long generations of privilege,

who rejected the standard professions and turned instead to arts and letters. "Those were the days when young men, job-hunting, wore frock coats and top hats to make an impression even in a newspaper office." Flower in buttonhole, linen immaculately fresh, bottoms of trousers rolled, they undertook to turn literature itself into a profession in a country whose view of the intellect remained pretty much what it had been in Tocqueville's day.

Brooks did not invent a melodrama, then, when he fancied himself faced by frying-pan and fire. And he made a self-conscious and brave choice: "the question was therefore how to change the whole texture of life at home so that writers and artists might develop there." All tremulous with misgiving he took on the truly formidable task, as Sherman Paul has observed, of making America Europe. Or, said in the terminology Brooks had devised, he would bring ideal and real, visionary imagination of the Germanic kind and cogency of systematic thought of the rationalist French sort, into a new and radically American balance. Returning to this country at a time of "Arctic loneliness for American writers," perhaps he would escape the sort of wreckage his own family suffered. In order to escape wreckage he would repress the will to escape: "submission is the price of peace."

This decision, a thing of high drama, was less momentous for American literature than the acolyte of art could have imagined and far more portentous for his inner life than he could have foreseen. Embracing a flimsy but plausible notion —deracination meant ruin—he returned to America almost in Puritanic renunciation of his deepest want. As is well known but ill understood, the scheme worked from 1914 when it was completed until 1925 when it and Brooks himself collapsed. In virtual textbook display of what Freud called the return of the repressed, Brooks in breakdown was haunted by the apparition of Henry James, by nightmares in which James "turned great luminous menacing eyes upon me." It was the figure of James that turned the screw of nightmare in the late twenties. But many years earlier, in childhood, it had been not James but a Hindu who appeared in the "earliest dream I remember," a "dream of flight." On the lawn a Hindu suddenly appeared, dressed in a suit of many colors, and chased the child Van Wyck with a knife. Just as he approached, running, "I soared into the air and floated away, free, aloft and safe. On other occasions, the fiend was not an Oriental, he was merely a nondescript minatory figure that pursued me, and I was not even anxious when I saw him approaching, for I knew I possessed the power to float away." That power—flight—deserted Brooks during the years of crisis when his intricately conceived scheme to evade wreckage was itself wrecked. And that figure, neither Oriental nor nondescript but now a most elegant avatar of deracination, of ruin, terrified Brooks with the minatory lesson: he who would evade himself is lost.*

If this seems too fanciful a proposition, consider the trope to which Brooks resorted in all moments of crisis throughout his life, the image of seafaring, of journeying through troubled waters. It appears first in a pamphlet *The Soul*, printed in San Francisco in 1910 and dedicated to his "maestro," that old seafarer John Butler Yeats, the poet's father. Subtitled "An Essay Toward a Point of View," it is composed of some forty gnomic, Emersonian paragraphs on the transcendent subject, art. The genius of poetry, that "ancient companion of the human soul," is its capacity to console: "in literature, I seemed to see a refuge . . . here was a kind of vicarious life which demanded no consistency of me, never demanded that I should be one thing at the expense

---

* Henry A. Murray, the psychiatrist and man of letters, figured among the considerable number of noted physicians to whom Brooks's family turned during the time of illness. I have no way of knowing the effect of Murray's advice on either Brooks or his family but, perhaps in coincidence, Murray years later (1955) published an essay called "American Icarus." It described the fantasies of a Harvard undergraduate who envisioned himself rising into the air, floating, flying, shooting through space. Murray proposed a new concept, the Icarus complex, as a way of characterizing emotional states connected with these fantasies. The Icarus complex represents an amalgam of "ascensionism," bursts of enthusiasm, "extravagant flights of fancy and rapid elevations of confidence," with an anticipation and fear of uncontrollable and unwanted descent. See Daniel M. Ogilvie's account in "The Icarus Complex," *Psychology Today*, 2:31–34, 67 (December 1968).

of another." Safe harbor too, literature, for a man to whom in fantasy human existence appeared as a "vast ocean which contained all things known and unknown . . . without a bottom." The lives of men, "like so many ships," were "sailing, tacking, drifting across the ocean. Some sailed swiftly . . . as if they steered for a distant shore: but this ocean had no shore." Now and then a pilot would drop a line into that bottomless sea and as it struck he "would take his bearings from this depth, supposing it to be the bottom. But this bottom was in reality, though he did not know it, only the wreckage of other ships floating near the surface." Then with a startling reversal of intent in what was conceived as a fantasy of consolation, Brooks says, "I will be this ocean: and if I have to be a ship I will be only a raft for the first wave to capsize and sink." That is to say, he would settle for nothing less than absolute literary triumph but he anticipated, feared, cataclysmic defeat.

Given this expectation of disaster, it is understandable that similar thoughts and images should have tortured him during that "time in the middle twenties when my own bubble burst. . . . What had I been doing? I had only ploughed the sea." The wretchedness of those years is understated in Brooks's published reminiscence but the letters, especially certain exchanges between Eleanor Brooks and Lewis Mumford, record a state of sheerest horror all around. I must refer again to this unhappy matter, for it is a storehouse of images which connect Brooks's writings with the lower depths of Brooks's mind. By 1929, indeed, he seemed to be beyond salvation, intent on perpetual flight from whatever demons pursued him, as Mrs. Brooks came to understand. Responding to a suggestion of Mumford's, she was forced to retract an earlier opinion of her husband's readiness for psychoanalytic treatment. He had always distrusted psychoanalysis and felt that it had injured people he knew—James Oppenheim for example. And although Brooks had said that he would be glad to be analyzed by Jung what he had really wanted, she discovered, was to leave America. And he had seized on Zürich as an excuse. Having had to pull him back from the front of trains and automobiles, she had decided that the act of uprooting him would be traumatic beyond bearing. Thoroughly "bedevilled," Brooks was later to say in print, he had seen himself as a "capsized ship with the passengers drowned underneath and the keel in the air. I could no longer sleep."

3

My Evil Tendency

> But the epitaph of his own criticism is long overdue: A purblind, morbid, theory-ridden metaphorician, in the name of creation, he led a multitude into the wastes of sterility and confusion.—Seward Collins, 1930

For five years he was unable to rest or work. Before then, from 1915 to 1925, he had achieved renown as the most metaphysical mind, the most urbane and eloquent voice, the most poised and coherent theorist of diverse movements in literary nationalism which flourished in the day of Resurgence.* First with a group of pacifist, Woodrow Wilsonian radicals on the *Seven Arts*—Bourne, Waldo Frank, Oppenheim, Paul Rosenfeld—and later as literary editor of Albert Jay Nock's paper, the *Freeman,* he acquired unparalleled authority among American intellectuals committed to one or another program of literary reform. Beginning in 1915 with *America's Coming-of-Age,* he contrived to sail a brave course across the "Saragasso Sea" of American

---

* Brooks's friends all along predicted for him a great career. Wheelock —writing to Eleanor Stimson (June 12, 1907) in congratulations on her engagement to Brooks—said that he and others were delighted that their friend was to be in London, doing the work of criticism which he had set himself to do, because a proper beginning to his literary life was of the highest importance. Without question, Wheelock remarked, Brooks was launched on a career which would most certainly have considerable effect: so ambitious, so resolute, so unselfish and so gifted was he that recognition must come in the course of time. And indeed his moment of highest prestige came barely ten years after Wheelock's prophecy.

literary and social history, that "prodigious welter of unconscious life, swept by ground-swells of half-conscious emotion . . . and unchecked, uncharted, unorganized vitality
like that of the first chaos." Then came *Letters and Leadership* (1918), the noted essay introducing Bourne's posthumous *History of a Literary Radical* (1920), and the last
of these studies in "The Literary Life of America" (1921)
which coincided with the appearance of Brooks's climactic
work on Mark Twain and Henry James. At mid-decade,
barely forty, he had acquired national eminence as the leading spokesman for the Beloved Community, as the harshest
critic of his generation, remorseless in his attack on a society
which sacrificed the creative life in favor of the acquisitive
life. Unlike H. L. Mencken, who chose the easy target of
official Philistine culture, Brooks assailed his colleagues
for having assisted at their own sacrifice. Jolted by and
thankful for this shock of recognition, they had presented
him with the Dial Award (for service to American letters)
and an offer of the editorship of that distinguished magazine,
and in print expressed their gratitude—unqualified, as in
Mary Colum's essay, qualified as in Paul Rosenfeld's,
Edmund Wilson's and Gorham Munson's—for his labors
in their behalf.

Single-handed, he had invented new tactics of navigation
which, it seemed, might serve to guide lost voyagers home.
Having returned from Europe to America as from frying pan
to fire, he introduced into his native land a vision of letters
and leadership developed in the course of his European
studies. Naturally none of his colleagues knew that the
deliverer was himself desperate for deliverance. No one
realized that Brooks hoped to find in imaginative literature
a harbor safe from the brutish Philistinism of American life.
Rather they cherished Brooks's criticism as still another
vivid example of the general revival of learning.

In truth, Brooks himself gave no exterior sign of discontent. Having moved to Westport, Connecticut, in 1920, he
shared in a general impulse of that moment, a wish to "draw
a secret strength from the old Yankee farmers who had oc-
cupied and tilled the land before them," his autobiography

says, and in this way to bring to a close the years of displacement. Although it took him more than twenty years, a longer immersion than he had anticipated, to live down his homesickness for Europe, his external life gave scarcely a clue that Westport did not fulfill his dream of Arcadia. And indeed it was in many ways a gratifying time. For these first years of the twenties coincided with the period of his editorship at the *Freeman* where, from 1920 to 1924 he wrote a weekly page called "A Reviewer's Notebook." In this space he pursued the themes which his first half-dozen books introduced, which the *Seven Arts* broadcast and which the studies of Mark Twain and Henry James proclaimed.

In that weekly essay, Brooks assumed the Delphic office. Ostensibly a reviewer of recent books — selections from Robert Ingersoll's speeches, James Huneker's *Steeplejack* — he transformed each review into a characteristic sermon on his habitual preoccupations: Ingersoll's supposedly dangerous Free Thought had been a village atheism, like Mark Twain's, and had served as a mere safety valve of repressiveness. Huneker's talent had withered because it lacked a proper soil to grow in and right gardeners to tend it. Brooks managed, as Gorham Munson said, to write on nearly all imaginable problems of American intellectual life without focusing his mind on the very labor which could sustain his judgment, the labor of literary analysis. What Brooks did concentrate on, brilliantly, was the work of comforting and sustaining the forces of opposition to Philistia during the time when the twenties generation went through its expatriate half-decade.

Half-consciously, he set himself two specific goals. He would continue the work begun in the period just before the war — that is, he would pursue the effort to create an imposing literary generation which, unified and determined, might establish a powerful literary epoch. "What constitutes a real generation in literature is, no doubt, the emergence and dominance of some one writer, of two or three writers perhaps, powerful enough to impose their ideas upon the mass. When a writer is great enough, it is impossible for those who grow up under his shadow to escape from his authority; as long as his genius remains active, he sets his stamp upon the whole spiritual life of his immediate successors." Whether or not Brooks fancied himself in this role—as Eliot at about the same time imagined a similar role for himself—Brooks's audience recognized his fitness for this Johnsonian office. What Brooks did clearly hope to contrive, however—that second of his goals—was an epoch in which American poets, recalled to their proper function, would serve as the unacknowledged legislators of the world.

And indeed Brooks's fame did represent a matchless moment of coalescence between the man and the epoch. Nowhere else and at no other time could he have found an audience more responsive to that tour de force of cost accounting with which he sought to discredit a society whose bond was underwritten by the law of profit and loss. His enterprise coincided with a general attack on the outrages of capitalism, with a rising labor movement, with an emerging Socialist party. Brooks, a socialist-pacifist who shared Wilson's sense of mission, hoped to inspire, to exhort the American people to fulfill its destiny by presenting to the international community of nations a model of disinterested service to mankind. Simultaneously, he himself presented to the nation at large and to a special circle of rebel-intellectuals in small, a bill of particulars listing the reasons why Americans would be hard pressed to realize Wilson's program. Conflict within the national consciousness thus coincided with polarity of will within Brooks's own consciousness. Out of conflict and polarity came a new vocabulary of antithesis which persuaded his audience that here at last was the oracle they had all been waiting for.

Composing those works which, as Mary Colum said, helped to create "the conditions in which the artist can work and flourish as a free spirit," he discovered in classic American letters "two main currents running side by side but rarely mingling." Embodied in Jonathan Edwards and Ben Franklin, that same rift continued to define causes of conflict down to the present day, Brooks maintained. In America "human nature itself exists on two irreconcilable planes"; its poetry, deprived of organic life, is therefore denied the right to fulfill its true office. In contrast to Europe, where art is the source of rapture and where artists mediate between the material and the spiritual life of man, Americans prefer the state of rupture. Two kinds of public, "the cultivated public and the business public," pursue divergent tastes which perpetually widen the gulf that separates them. The highbrow public exists on the plane of "stark intellectuality" and the lowbrow public exists on the plane of "stark business," of money-grabbing and flag-waving.* Under these conditions poetry cannot harness thought and action, cannot transform the great American experiment "into a disinterested adventure." Brooks, having come this distance by way of his customary route—the language of dualism—ended his essay, *Letters and Leadership*, with his characteristic imagery. "So becalmed as we are on a rolling sea, flapping and fluttering, hesitating and veering about, oppressed with a faint nausea, is it strange that we have turned mutinous?"

Composing the *Three Essays on America*, Brooks set out to isolate and specify the twin traditions of thought in America. Simultaneously, he sought to prepare the way for a guild of artists, men of "exalted soul" who would fuse the life of poetry with the life of action: America, unified at last, would realize its old dream of utopia.* But before this program of salvation could be properly carried forward, its

---

* It is startling, too, to find Brooks in *The Freeman* citing Lowes Dickinson's portrait of the American as Enemy—and to discover how frighteningly apt today this portrait is: "masterful, aggressive, unscrupulous, egotistic, at once good-natured and brutal, kind if you do not cross him, ruthless if you do, greedy, ambitious, self-reliant, active for the sake of activity, intelligent and unintellectual, quick-witted and crass, contemptuous of ideas but amorous of devices, valuing nothing but success . . . the master of methods and slave of things and therefore the conqueror of the world." This accomplished brute, Brooks concluded, shifting from Dickinson's voice to his own, has taken "possession of the popular mind, in all its suggestibility, and filled it with its own appetites."

* The manuscript of *America's Coming-of-Age*, handwritten, contains two telling statements which do not appear in print, a subtitle and an epigraph. "The American Myth" was Brooks's first choice for his subtitle; "Nothing great has been established which does not rest on a legend," from Renan's *Life of Jesus*, was intended to stand as an epigraph for the whole book.

theory wanted testing. And Brooks conceived a trilogy of books on classic American writers, Mark Twain and Henry James and Whitman, which would exhibit the full effects of all those patterns of disjunction—of wine and the aroma of wine, of French temper and German, of rhetoric and poetry, of real and ideal, of lowbrow and highbrow—he had traced during more than a decade's study. The books on Mark Twain and James would exhibit the consequences of lowbrow debasement and highbrow attenuation of spirit in American literature. And a final book would present Whitman as the very model of a perfect poet, a very Antaeus of a man who "for the first time, gave us the sense of something organic in American life." Brooks substituted Emerson for Whitman, so the story goes, when he learned of Whitman's homosexuality. Indeed he was so upset on hearing this at lunch with Malcolm Cowley in the Harvard Club that he left the table immediately. Cowley tells the story. And another of Brooks's friends, Theodore Maynard, says it was probably he who suggested Emerson.

However that may be, the revised project was greeted by members of his circle as the proper work of a man whose learning and eloquence was more than equal to the labor of representing what was then called the Young Generation in its debate with received opinion. And indeed by 1925 Brooks had accomplished sheer rout. He dispelled virtually overnight a whole tribe of university scholars who conducted literary affairs according to laws of taste which excluded the new criticism, the new poetry, the new painting—the new age. Reading Stuart Pratt Sherman on Mark Twain, Bourne told Brooks in a letter (March 1917), "made me chortle with joy at the thought of how much you are going to show him when you get started. You simply have no competition." Sherman simply "hasn't an idea in the world that Mark Twain was anything more than a hearty, healthy vulgarian. . . . But you will change all that when you get started."

The book with which he stirred the younger and outraged the older generation was *The Ordeal of Mark Twain*. Despite the fury this work roused among ritual cultists of Clemens, the *Ordeal* remains a compelling book. Securely placed among specialist studies of Mark Twain, its place among benchmark books in another kind of literature is perhaps less secure but more imposing. For all its humorlessness, its ax-grinding and thesis-mongering, the *Ordeal* bore some marvelous first fruits of inquiry into the connections between neurosis and art, unconscious motive and literary act. And particularly as it raised some radical questions about the discontents of civilization in the United States, questions which its chief critic Bernard DeVoto failed to discredit, has it earned its fame and proved its worth. Now that we are untroubled by its success or failure in creating a literary school, by its crudeness of formulation or its hyperbole of judgment, perhaps we can properly admire this imperfect book for the risks it took, the intellectual and moral passion it displayed, the energy it generated.

Mark Twain was no frontiersman of American jollity, Brooks argued, but was deep down afflicted by a "malady of the soul, a malady common to many Americans." His "unconscious desire was to be an artist; but this implied an assertion of individuality that was a sin in the eyes of his mother and a shame in the eyes of society." In fact the "mere assertion of individuality" was a menace to the integrity of "the herd," incarnate in that mother who "wanted him to be a businessman." This "eternal dilemma of every American writer" Mark Twain solved by choosing the mode of comedy even though he felt that as a humorist he was "selling rather than fulfilling his soul." His "original unconscious motive" for surrendering his creative life had been an oath, taken at his father's deathbed, to succeed in business in order to please his mother, Jane Clemens. This first surrender had been followed by another, to his wife Olivia, who imposed on her "shorn Samson" the prissy rules, sterile tastes, and vacant intelligence of the genteel tradition. Until then surrender had been half not wholehearted. But when he married Olivia his life took permanent shape. Then it was that he resorted to an unconscious strategy which enabled him to cope with the "domestic diet of Mrs. Clemens, the literary diet of Mr. Howells, those second parents who had taken the place of the first." Mark Twain, as his somnambulism indicates, became a "dual personality."

Somnambulism, gloom, obsession with double identity— these represent the effects of a "repressed creative instinct" which it is "death to hide." Repressed, Mark Twain's "wish to be an artist" was supplanted by another, less agreeable but inexpungeable want: to win public approval and acquire great wealth by conforming to public opinion. The impulse to conform clashed with the impulse to resist. Brooks contended that this struggle, which implicated two competing wishes or "groups of wishes"—expressed in *Pudd'nhead Wilson* and *The Prince and the Pauper* as a struggle between two selves—undermined the genius of a man in whom "the poet, the artist, the individual" barely managed to survive. Because the poet lived on in cap and bells, the man managed to maintain a small measure of self-respect, to acquire high accolade and vast fortune, and preserve balance enough to outlast the despair which almost overcame him in the end. "I disseminate my true views," Mark Twain said in 1900, "by means of a series of apparently humorous and mendacious stories." The remark is given in Justin Kaplan's new biography, *Mr. Clemens and Mark Twain* (1966), and Mr. Kaplan adds that at this time in Mark Twain's life "fiction, dreams, and lies had become confused, and he could not tell them apart. They were all 'frankly and hysterically insane.'" Mr. Kaplan's is a fine book, incidentally, which dispenses both with Freud and, rather unkindly, with Brooks—even as it takes up, amplifies, modifies the thread of Brooks's thought. What was hastily argued in 1920 is pursued at leisurely pace in 1966: *Mr. Clemens and Mark Twain* ends with the old man at the instant before his final coma talking about "Jekyll and Hyde and dual personality."

On publication, *The Ordeal of Mark Twain* split its readers into two camps which engaged in guerrilla warfare until Bernard DeVoto in 1932, the year Brooks published a revised edition, offered in rebuttal *Mark Twain's America*. Accusing Brooks of having initiated a "fatally easy method of interpreting history," DeVoto condemned him for incompetence in psychoanalysis, for "shifting offhand from

Freud to Adler to Jung as each of them served his purpose" and (I refer to Stanley Edgar Hyman's view of the
affair) for "contradictions, distortions, misrepresentations,
and unwarranted assumptions on page after page." Following DeVoto nearly two generations of critics have taken up
the debate. It continues.* And in consequence today neither
Brooks's wholesale derogation of Mark Twain's genius nor
DeVoto's wholesale condemnation of Brooks's thesis is
quite acceptable. The question of Mark Twain's wound,
as the matter is now known, cannot be discounted. Nor can
the fact of Clemens's achievement be dismissed, explained
away.

Brooks's 1932 revision of the *Ordeal*, itself a product of
his own years of desperation, represents a retreat from some
hard-won positions. Far more ground was given up than is
accounted for in a simple arithmetic of words changed or
phrases dropped. This particular matter, comparison of texts,
has been amply studied and I shall not reproduce details.
It is true, however, that the ground he conceded was easily
surrendered, and its loss did not appease those of his critics
who admired the shape of his thought, as Gamaliel Bradford said in a letter (June 1923), but were distressed by the
way he had used Mark Twain as a mannequin to hang a
garment on. Brooks's tendency was to falsify—just a trifle
maybe, Bradford agreed, but a trifle all the same. Brooks responded with an apology and a promise: he was very keenly
aware of his evil tendency to impose a thesis. The
Mark Twain suffered from this, he recognized, but the
Henry James will not—even if he had to spend another two
years on the book.

The Pilgrimage of Henry James was to be an exercise in
many kinds of self-discipline but it would confirm, not correct, iniquity. Brooks wrote both books in barely muted

* Debate continues, indeed, as does more or less unmodified the
general complaint against Brooks's amateur psychologizing: "Brooks's
eclectic use of psychology [leads him to offer] the reader a choice of
psychological explanations" both "semi-Freudian" and Adlerian, we
learn in a quite recent study of the old problem, an eclecticism of
psychologic machinery which is "both confusing and cumbersome."
Claudia C. Morrison *Freud and the Critic*. Chapel Hill: University of
North Carolina Press, 1968, p. 183.

stridency of distaste for America, in an unrecognized and unwelcome ecstasy of longing for Europe. But the *Ordeal* was irretrievable for another, plainer reason. Having used Mark Twain as a mannequin, Brooks had simply lifted its skeleton from Hart's book on insanity. He was therefore simply unable to accomplish the sort of radical revision which friendly critics would have admired. And since he chose not to identify Hart as his source of psychological learning, he left his critics to make out, with good guess and bad, the origins and ends of his thought. "Like the Freudians," Alfred Kazin remarked, "Brooks was writing to a thesis; but it was not a Freudian thesis." Nor was it an idiosyncratic pastiche, as other critics complained. It was Hart's composite portrait of the life of the psyche, Hart's synthesis of four schools of psychological thought—Freud's, Janet's, Adler's, Jung's—which Brooks adapted to his study of Mark Twain's psychic life. And it could not be jettisoned.

I have already remarked Hart's habit of argument, his addiction to the principle of the "causal complex" and so on. But this does inadequate justice to the tightness of connection which binds *The Ordeal of Mark Twain* to *The Psychology of Insanity*. Here is one of those rare and fortuitous instances in the history of ideas when direct and presiding influence, one work on another, is incontrovertible. Reading Hart today, you can recapture a measure of the excitement Brooks must have felt as he found in this handbook the key which unlocked the riddle of Mark Twain's life, of the creative life in America. Here in this concise and authoritative book was all the information necessary to connect character and culture. In Hart's two chapters on "Repression" and "Manifestations of Repressed Complexes," he learned all the Freudian theory he needed to know in order to understand the principle of unconscious conflict. And in Hart's chapter on Janet, on "Dissociation," Brooks was given a ready-made system and language which accounted for some hitherto unaccountable traits of character.

The conception of dissociation enables us to represent the mental state of those patients, Hart said, whose delusions are impervious to facts. "They pursue their courses in logic-tight compartments, as it were, separated by barriers through which no connecting thought or reasoning is permitted to pass." One main form of dissociation was somnambulism; another was the commonly known one of "double personality." Illustrating the origins of somnambulism, Hart used an example offered by Janet: Irène, a young woman whose mother's death had been peculiarly painful, developed "an abnormal mental condition" whose symptoms resembled "those exhibited by the ordinary sleepwalker." Irène "would live through the deathbed scene again and again, her whole mind absorbed in the phantasy, and altogether oblivious of what was actually taking place around her."

What a thrill of recognition Brooks must have felt as he sorted out Hart's ideas, took what he needed, then reshaped Hart's pattern to match the design of Mark Twain's life and art. Retelling Albert Bigelow Paine's version of the deathbed oath—to which Brooks clung even though Paine's account, relying as it did solely on Mark Twain's recollections, was a notoriously unreliable report of what Mark Twain chose to remember or misremember—Brooks let out the stops. "That night—it was after the funeral—his tendency to somnambulism manifested itself." It is "perfectly evident what happened to Mark Twain at this moment: he became, and his immediate manifestation of somnambulism is the proof of it, a dual personality." The only reason why earlier generations of critics had neglected this proof was their ignorance of psychology. Now that psychology has made us "familiar with the principle of the 'water-tight compartment,'" we realize that Mark Twain was the "chronic victim of a mode of life that placed him bodily and morally in one situation after another where, in order to survive he had to violate the law of his own spirit." Having submitted to his mother's will, he assumed the character and attitudes of a "typical American magnate." His transformation into a "money-making, wire-pulling Philistine," saddled him with a "dissociated self" which was permanently at odds with his "true individuality."

In explanation of the reasons for Mark Twain's submission, Brooks relied on Hart's paraphrase of ideas drawn from another prestigious work of the time, W. Trotter's *The Instincts of the Herd in Peace and War*. Trotter demonstrates the existence of a fourth instinct, Hart said, "of fundamental importance in the psychology of gregarious animals," a herd instinct which "ensures that the behaviour of the individual shall be in harmony with that of the community as a whole. Owing to its action each individual tends to accept without question the beliefs which are current in his class, and to carry out with unthinking obedience the rules of conduct upon which the herd has set its sanction." It will be immediately obvious, Hart concluded, that in "these struggles between the primary instincts and the beliefs and codes enforced by the operation of the herd instinct, we have a fertile field for mental conflict." What Trotter called herd Freud called superego. But Hart preferred Trotter to Freud on this subject, and Brooks followed Hart. It is immediately obvious, Brooks observed, how repression of Mark Twain's creative instinct was accompanied by the rise "to the highest degree" of his "acquisitive instinct, the race instinct." His individuality sacrifices itself, "loses itself in the herd," and in the end becomes the supreme victim of that epoch in American history, the pioneer, when "one was required not merely to forego one's individual tastes and beliefs and ideas but positively cry up the beliefs and tastes of the herd."

Obviously Brooks's thesis was neither Freudian nor a pastiche of Freud and someone else. *The Psychology of Insanity* provided a system of ideas on individual and social behavior which Brooks absorbed, paraphrased, and exploited in his programmatic study of both Mark Twain and Henry James. It was a matter of lock, stock, and barrel. To have tampered with this system would have been to dismember Hart's thought. Revising the *Ordeal*, Brooks could correct a howler or two, tone down or play up: pure cosmetics. Besides, there was no particular reason to doubt Hart's word or to suspect that the close analysis of Mark Twain's life or Henry James's art did not substantiate Hart's eclectic psychology.

Before he abandoned the psychology of literature, he undertook to complete the second volume in his trilogy of biographies of standard American authors. It had always been his intention to write a three-book series in which the third volume would be "a sort of *Paradiso,* after what I conceived to be the *Inferno* of Mark Twain and the *Purgatorio* of Henry James." Strange fruit of the Harvard cult of Dante. Composing *The Pilgrimage of Henry James* he set out to examine the validity of James's assumption that the artist cannot thrive in the American atmosphere. In this way he would fulfill a holy mission, as he told Bradford: he would rescue James from the Jacobites and show that James spoke the sober truth about the immense fascination of England (as applied to himself, that is) and in consequence of what Brooks believed were certain weaknesses in James's own nature.*

In order to rescue James, Brooks was compelled to show that the great man, confronting frying pan and fire, had deliberately chosen the frying pan, Europe. The choice had been a bad one but James's judgment of the fire's heat had been accurate indeed. For James was "the first novelist in the distinctively American line of our day: the first to challenge the herd-instinct, to reveal the inadequacy of our social life, to present the plight of the highly personalized human being in the primitive community." Unlike Brooks, who immersed himself in the primitive American community, who exposed himself to fire, who fought it out with the "herd"—James fled. Flying, he "lost the basis of a novelist's life." He laid down a siege of London, won the war, lost himself. English society cut him "in two" and the public Henry James emerged, a "vast arachnid of art, pouncing

---

* This belief dates from Brooks's boyhood, his schoolboyhood at The Seminary where, in 1903, writing to Eleanor Stimson, he described a distaste which was to be lifelong: "I don't know much about Henry James, except that he's a brother of Prof. James, of Harvard, is an infernal snob, and *does* know how to write English. His books are very psychological, aren't they? His brother is the greatest psychologist in the world. I think Henry James was the reprobate who wrote Daisy Miller. Read that and you won't think much of him. He lives in Europe in a sort of William-Waldorf-Astor style."

upon the tiny air-blown particle and wrapping it round and round." Like Amiel, James spun large circles around the tiniest molecules of nuance. This was the James adored by the Jacobites, the Old Pretender whose play of style, a "mind working in the void," represented the ruin of art. Tracing ruin to James's deracination, Brooks concluded that a writer without a country of his own must sink in "the dividing sea."

The *Pilgrimage of Henry James* is better than its reputation, as F. W. Dupee said thirty years ago. Even when "in his main argument he appears most mistaken," his book attests his passion to raise and resolve crucial problems. That Brooks is mistaken in his judgment of James's art is unarguable—not because James's fiction is faultless but because it is the superb instrument of a man whose genius lay in the spheres of irony. And Brooks's theory, which combined a sociology of rhetoric with a psychology of poetry, drove him to exclude irony. To start on a quest in search of Henry James, Edna Kenton said in a review, "with a theory strapped to one's feet instead of winged curiosity poised within the mind," is disastrous. Accused of having committed grave errors of procedure—undocumented partial quotation, muddled paraphrase—Brooks caused his reviewers to wonder, Where was truth.

Mark Twain the infernal lowbrow and James the expurgated highbrow were victims of a civilization which it was Brooks's holy mission to reform. This was all the truth he cared about, his Dantesque vision of America. Perhaps, too, the study of James was intended to serve as a lesson in self-admonition at the very moment in the twenties when the fascination of Europe was irresistible to nearly all Americans. Having denied himself that refuge, Brooks had chosen literature as his safe harbor. But suddenly, shortly after he published this book, his ship capsized. And during the next five years as Eleanor Brooks and Lewis Mumford consulted physicians, enlisted friends, desperate for an effective way to restore Brooks to himself, he went from asylum to asylum in search of extinction, haunted by Henry James.

Until this time of crisis he had said momentous things

about the nature of conflict between literary generations and within the social and literary imagination in America. He had pursued a course parallel to that staked out for him by Edmund Wilson in a letter (March 1921), which remarked on the enormous need for someone to do for the American Victorian age what Lytton Strachey had accomplished for the English. In Wilson's judgment, the *Mark Twain* had represented a magnificent first step along that path. Out of Brooks's divided mind had come a stirring —though hyperbolic—account of polarity in the national experience. Invariably his mind had centered on divorce, split, pairs of duelling wills. And it had concentrated attention on the disabling effects of disjunction inside single persons and within social systems. Arguing Brooks's way, Hart's way, we can say that a "causal complex" in the man explains an obsession with antinomianism in the world. In response to this obsession, he had invented an ingenious vocabulary of antithesis, had analyzed diverse forms of dualism in England, on the Continent, and in America where, at last, he addressed to the Young Generation a full-fledged psychology, sociology, and philosophy of literary reform. A guild of evangels, these men and women would create a poetics of the body politic which would harness art and action.

Out of duality, singleness; out of diversity, unity; out of unity, wholeness; out of organic wholeness, order; out of order, utopia—this sequence of ideas served as the theme of Brooks's rhetoric until 1925.* One fixed idea suffused the lot. Drawn from German and the English Romanticism, it proclaimed that the creative life, the life of art, the artist's stubborn instinct for self-realization—"self-effectuation,"

---

* Malcolm Cowley, in a letter of October 8, 1964, insists that "VWB *wasn't* a utopian. Neither was he a millennialist, or in any measure chiliastic. The word 'utopia' has a false and somewhat supercilious connotation. . . . Brooks was a meliorist, that is, a believer in human improvability (not perfectability), specifically by means of literature, with writers as leaders by example." Although Cowley's opinion is I think mistaken, the matter is indeed not open-and-shut. I trust that it is absolutely clear that I write with no condescension or superciliousness.

Brooks said—must inspire individual beings to resist the herd. In this way the artist in America, Emerson's Orphic poet incarnate, would furnish all mankind with an exemplary figure of obstinate honor and untrammeled will.

4

A Cold Black Draughty Void

In the several volumes of his memoirs and in the unpublished material, he has offered himself as a case history of a writer's education, social life, and creative psychopathology. . . . Scattered here and there in literature are small texts that ought to be gathered together as a sort of Bible for young writers, ignorant of both the best and the worst that is before them . . . a sort of pharmacopeia for middle-aged writers who, for some reason, have lost their powers and their faith in literature.—Glenway Wescott, 1964

Brooks's timing could not have been worse. He arrived at this stage of thought at the moment least auspicious for its exaltation. During the war years, vast varieties of hope, gathered under the rubric of Wilsonian idealism, had come to little. War had killed the *Seven Arts*; strain of will and gloom of spirit along with influenza had killed Randolph Bourne. And it was at this grim time of general disillusion that Brooks, completing his allegory, found himself at a loss. Unable to visualize that heaven which his prophecy had forecast, he was left with rhetoric alone. By 1925, when anybody in his right mind could see that an artist could readily thrive virtually anywhere outside the United States, Brooks found himself utterly unable to contend that Emerson has prospered in an American atmosphere. Having proved that an artist is doomed if he stays here and damned if he leaves, having arbitrarily decided, for consistency's sake, that Emerson not Whitman would embody the triumph of American genius—having shifted from Whitman whom he adored to Emerson whom he had earlier half-reviled as dried manna of Concord—Brooks reached exactly that state of impasse he had observed in Symonds's life. First cul-de-sac, then breakdown. Having negotiated the inferno, scaled purgatorio, he found himself stalled at the gates of paradise.

In the state of emotional collapse which followed we can discern some strange but telling conjunctions between Brooks's Dantesque allegory of the American soul, its progress from damnation to salvation, and Brooks's despair. In breakdown, his whole terror was fixed on the certainty of reprobation. Speaking with one of his closest friends, the scientist-adventurer-writer Hans Zinsser, come East from California to consult and advise, Brooks tried to convince Zinsser that he, Brooks, was doomed to die of starvation in jail. In that panic time of guilt and self-accusation, he foresaw one sure end: punishment in hell. In 1928 he asked Zinsser to kill him. Much later, in autobiography, he was able to turn terror into a figure of speech, "Season in Hell," but in the late twenties he had no taste for conceit. What had begun as a term of rhetoric had become infernally real.

A man who accuses himself of crimes he does not commit must surely be convinced he is condemned for some reason. When we remember that Brooks, a man of Puritanic conscience—a conscience that was like a cancer, as he said in another connection—was terrorized by the apparition of Henry James, we cannot be far wrong if we guess that Brooks feared retribution induced by his "evil tendency" to falsify, to impose a thesis. And no advice could redeem regret or could assuage guilt or diminish the sense of evil. Advice of various kinds, from Brooks's large circle of friends, was bountifully given, gratefully received, and found wanting. Mary Colum, for example, later told Brooks that it had been Scofield Thayer, the editor of the *Dial*, who had first warned her how ill Brooks was. Mrs. Colum recalled that she had told Thayer that Brooks was well enough but Thayer should look to himself. Shortly afterward, he collapsed, retired from the *Dial*, from the world. Mrs. Colum also told Brooks that in 1927 in Paris, she had spoken with

Pierre Janet—the theorist of dissociation on whom Brooks
had drawn for his *Mark Twain*—and Janet had said that
Brooks's cure hinged on an end of meditation, of inquiry into
the laws of his own inner being and into the inner nature of
all other general laws of whatever kind.

This was, in any event, apparently the plan of attack in
treatment devised in an English sanitarium, Harrow-on-the-
Hill, where Brooks was to spend eight months during the
mid-twenties. A letter written to his wife shortly after his
arrival there is worth reproducing in full—for the folly of
treatment, given Brooks's sort of character, intended to replace old habits of hard thought with new habits of reso-
lutely English outdoorsy play. "I haven't really described to
you yet the life in this house. I am going on in a sort of routine and as I'm not allowed out of Harrow I really having
nothing else very much to tell you about. It is a perfectly
heavenly place . . . on the top of a hill, with great elms
(not at all like our elms but more like oaks in shape, etc.),
mulberry trees and I don't know what else. There is a long
slope below, with grazing cattle, etc. . . . a rose garden
and a tennis court at the bottom of the lawn. Then, at the
back of the house, a walled vegetable garden, presided over
by a Mr. Wade, a former patient who has become a member
of the staff, like a 'big brother' in a monastery. He directs
the tennis, takes everybody about on walks, etc. There is
also a workshop, where one does carpentry, leather-work,
brass-work, etc. Everybody is supposed to work in the morning and play in the afternoon—the play mainly tennis,
though there is also a putting-green and sometimes we go
swimming in a municipal pool about 2 miles away. Of course,
the tennis is 'work' for me, & pretty disagreeable work, but
they think it most important that I should learn this—and
I think I *am* learning it.

(Don't tell Charlie anything about these exploits. I want
to appear before him as a good player and mean to learn to
do so.) I can already serve the balls into the right court 3
times out of 5 and am getting better at returning the balls.
I am also trying to learn to dive—which I find a horrible
business. Day before yesterday I made my second crude at-

tempt, jumped off upside down and *hit the bottom* of the 7-foot end. No harm done. I shall learn to go in slantwise the proper way before I get through, if there is time before they close the pool for the summer at the end of the month. Some of the people are awfully nice, some of the others are awfully queer. There is an epileptic woman who woke me up at 1 o'clock this morning by having a ghastly fit with screams overhead. A good many Scotch and some Irish people. One or two *very pretty women*—but unfortunately with stalwart & devoted husbands who come to see them at intervals. On Saturday P.M. we play baseball—a queer imitation of our game at home—with a very small diamond and a big ball—almost like a punching-bag. On Sundays we all walk to church in the late A.M. . . . . [a] 14th century church about 2 miles away. Next for my schedule: I am still left in bed till 10 A.M. & have to take some kind of medicine (I'm not told what it is) three times a day. At 10:30 Swedish exercise, with goose-step, etc., on the tennis court. Then work in the garden or carpenter-shop till lunch-time. In the afternoon, much tennis. Everybody is so obviously kind here—I never knew such good people—and as it's supposed to be very important for me to learn to play tennis they are tiring themselves out to give me practise—in singles or doubles. At 4:30 tea. In the evening, 3 times a week, dancing, and then how I wish you were here to dance with! The other evenings, bridge. I am resigned to these damned games and I *hope* I shall learn to like playing them. I can't explain the reasons why these things are supposed to be so important in my case. It's too complicated, till I see you. But I *understand why*. The doctor is the best & wisest man I ever met. He knows human nature inside out; and is so amusing too. I'm writing this letter in bed, & must get up now & run to the bathroom and get ready for the exercises. O my darling how I hope everything is all right with you. With all my love and a hug for the boys."

Very soon it was clear that gardening and games could not relieve him of—and I suspect may have heightened—the delusion that his wise doctor had induced Parliament to pass a special bill permitting them, at Harrow, to bury him alive in a small chamber. He was in fact entombed there: a rest cure so appallingly vacant was indeed a living death for a man of his sensibility. And of course it failed to erase from the grooves of his mind two decades worth of speculative thought, of meditation on the laws governing the creative life in Europe and America. Fortunately, Mrs. Brooks received other advice. William A. White, another distinguished psychiatrist, told her that Brooks should be urged to complete the book on Emerson. Indeed, apart from Janet, everyone was convinced that Brooks would be miraculously restored to health if only he could finish that third volume. If the Emerson succeeds, Mrs. Brooks wrote to Mumford, he will be cured. Only Brooks himself was unconvinced. In 1928, responding to a request from Norman Foerster to contribute to the volume *Humanism in America* he said that he simply had nothing to say. A year later Mrs. Brooks again suggested to her husband the idea of publishing portions of his work on Emerson. But he told her that there was nothing to publish. During this period he did manage to conduct some correspondence, to write two articles for the *Encyclopedia Brittanica,* and one for the *Dictionary of American Biography.*

The problem he alone understood and could not resolve—whatever his physicians, wife, friends said—was not simply how to get on with Emerson but how in heaven's name could he speak of salvation when he felt himself cast out, condemned, disgraced. That this feeling was unreasonable is hardly worth saying. The strongest complaint that anyone could register against his work was that it was tendentious or, as Gorham Munson in 1925 maintained, that his kind of social and "genetic" criticism too often substituted moral fervor for formal analysis. Everyone recognized in Brooks a dashing polemicist; what Brooks prized in himself was a Germanic foolhardiness of poetic intuition. And what drove him to distraction was loss of faith in his power of vision. The condition of life in America, he decided, was sheer hell from which there was no escape— neither in the classic American and paternal solution, flight to Europe, nor in immersion in private fancy. The only thing he could do was wait for the descent of that Hindu's knife, fit punishment for a faithless man.

External evidence in support of these speculations is scanty, but internal evidence is plentiful. For when *The Life of Emerson* (1932) did finally appear, it expressed no reassertion of faith, but rather displayed Mrs. Brooks's, Mumford's and the publisher's, Dutton's, faith in the healing power of love. This triumverate sought to do for Brooks what he was incapable of doing for himself, raise him from the slough of despond. Mumford's role is especially notable in that he performed a variety of literary tasks with exactly the kind of fidelity he brought to bear on multitudinous works of friendship during these hard years. For it was he who undertook to arrange for treatment by Jung, who assured Mrs. Brooks that money would not be permitted to interfere with therapy. Advising her that, contrary to Brooks's belief, the book was finished—that the final chapter summarizing Emerson's philosophy, could not be tacked on because it was incompatible with Brooks's intention to recreate the quality of Emerson's life by relying on Emerson's own words—Mumford worked to persuade everyone concerned with Brooks's affairs to go ahead with the book. "Believing that a financial lift would help Brooks's condition, and might make him willing to publish the work," Mumford says in a letter (September 6, 1968) intended to set right some statements I had made in print, "Maxwell Perkins and I approached Carl Van Doren and got him to accept it for the Literary Guild, without its having been offered to them by Dutton. (John Macrae, up to then, had been so irritated by having his offerings turned down by the two book clubs that he had vowed never to submit another manuscript to them: so we had, somehow, to break down both Brooks's resistance and Macrae's.) Van Doren, on his own responsibility, gallantly accepted the book; and after that, Brooks's acquiescence—and Macrae's too—was easy to achieve."

It is this book, momentous for its value in helping to restore Brooks's health, his first to have a wide popular sale, which both pleased and disconcerted its admirers. "Your pictures of Emerson are perfect in the way of expressions,"

Santayana wrote Brooks; "but just how much is quoted, and how much is your own?" *The Life of Emerson*, Stanley Hyman said, flatly, harshly, "marked the end of his serious work." Whether or not this book marked the end of Brooks's important work, it was the first of many books which exploited a style of work that marks the breach in Brooks's career. "Instead of thundering like a prophet," Cowley said in 1961—an essay which Mumford says that Brooks especially liked—"he became a scholar quoting unobtrusively from Emerson's writings and weaving together the quotations into an idyllic tapestry." Cowley is accurate indeed, and generous. But I suspect that Brooks adopted this method of composition in order to vanish from his book quite as, upon recovering from malaise, he banished from his mind any notion of completing his allegory.*

"May I say one further word about the method I have pursued," he was to comment in *Writer in America* (1953). Answering Santayana's question, responding to those critics who treated the five volumes of literary history as "a sort of irresponsible frolic or brainless joyride." Brooks described his method as that of a novelist whose every character, scene, and phrase were "founded on fact." But a more important word on method he left unsaid, its attribution to H. G. Wells whose habit of composition in 1914 he had cited and approved. "I make my beliefs as I want them,"

---

* This particular subject was indisputably of the first importance both to Brooks and his critics. And Brooks sought to have, even as he despaired of having, the last word. In the box holding his research notes to the *Opinions of Oliver Allston* (itself in manuscript called "Washington Allston"), he pasted a statement labelled "Notes for My History." He feared that it too would be misunderstood and would again cause him to be misrepresented: "Often, on a page with heading of somebody's biography or study, I note this author's ideas and then (without warning) go on with my own. It will appear that I have stolen my ideas. . . . Sometimes my own thoughts are placed on the same page with those of the author. Only I know which are which. Sometimes I copy out erroneous statements to remind myself to reply to them later." Anyone reading these notes, I am compelled to say, would find that the method involved risks of documentation and citation which were not worth taking—except perhaps as the technique enabled Brooks to weave himself into a tapestry where, like Joyce, he was everywhere present and nowhere visible.

Wells wrote. "I make them thus and not thus exactly as an artist makes a picture. . . . That does not mean I make them wantonly and regardless of fact." From Wells, Brooks learned to make brush strokes of the intuitive imagination which, he hoped, would lift the writing of history to the loftiest conceivable realm, the realm of visionary art.

The season in hell ended shortly before *The Life of Emerson* appeared. Why it came to an end, what discoveries or disclosures eased his spirit, Brooks's autobiography does not reveal. Brooks's family and friends agree that private financial crisis had triggered his despair. And it is clear from Brooks's correspondence that the matter of money, all during those painful, passionate, and occasionally distraught years preceding his marriage, had plagued him beyond reason. Even after he had returned to the world, in 1940, as Eleanor Brooks told Mumford, the sight of a bill always destroyed, temporarily, his ability to write. By then, however, the external problems had been pretty well resolved, as we learn from Charles Van Wyck Brooks, whose letter (October 22, 1968) describes the special arrangements which finally, in the early thirties, released his father from external causes of despair. "The fact is that my mother's rich relatives raised a sum of almost $100,000 as a trust fund for the two of them, and I do not doubt that this was the proximate cause of his recovery. His feelings must have remained very ambivalent about it. He could never bear to speak of money, and I never knew at any time at all what his finances were." Not really concerned to pry further—to go deeper is impossible and to speculate wider is unfair—I think the final word must be Brooks's own. "And even after I came back to life and sailed out clear and free I remained conscious at moments of an abyss beside me. I seemed to catch out of the tail of my eye a cold black draughty void, with a feeling that I stood on the brink of it in peril of my reason."

On emerging from the abyss, Brooks foreswore allegory. But he did not forego his intention to write an account—as he had promised Bradford in 1925 shortly before his collapse, when the book on Emerson was "flowing like distilled

honey"—of the "triumphantly successful literary life." Returning to the state of equipoise he set out, again ten-
dentiously, to replace the life of Emerson with the whole
"American pageant of genius." Having presented Emerson's
life by way of stylized paraphrases of Emerson's own words,
having found comfort in the state of anonymity which this
style conferred, he embarked on a major effort of literary
history, Makers and Finders (1936–55), which would "show
the interaction of American letters and life," would connect
"the literary present with the past," and would revive "the
special kind of memory that fertilizes the living mind and
gives it the sense of a base on which to build."

Beginning in the middle thirties, Brooks engaged in a
herculean labor of inquiry into the folklore and mythology
of the creative spirit in all spheres of the American imagination from its origins until the present day. He described this
project as a search for a usable past. His phrase stuck. Indeed, it is today no longer recognized as Brooks's phrase at
all and seems to represent a peculiarly American attitude
toward history itself, as Daniel Boorstin's An American
Primer and Henry Steele Commager's and Allen Nevins's
America: The Story of a Free People, attest. Strikingly, too,
the kind of censure registered against these books is identical to that registered against Brooks's The Flowering of New
England on its appearance in 1936. In accord with the
doctrine of a usable past, "American history has invariably
been written from Columbus to yesterday without the
slightest change of pace or tone," we read in the New
Statesman (June 2, 1967). The problem with this doctrine
is that it contains within itself the idea of "the disposable
past." Whatever does not fit goes to the scrap heap. It has
"no place in your 1968 Model Past."

Reading The Flowering of New England and New England: Indian Summer, first two of five volumes in Makers
and Finders, René Wellek in 1942 mourned the disappear-
ance of the old trenchancy of Brooks's mind, its replacement
with a "belletristic skill of patching together quotations,
drawing little miniatures, retelling anecdotes and describing
costumes and faces." Still harsher criticism was uniform

among a wide group of academic intellectuals which had been roused by Brooks's first books. "All my reading of American literature has been done during the era of Van Wyck Brooks and Parrington," Matthiessen said, but Brooks's new method of composition robbed history of its clash and struggle and so diluted the character of leading persons that it became hard to tell one man from another. However severe, these critics struggled to be just to the man who had revitalized their study of American themes. But even as they admired the very considerable merits of scholarship exhibited in these volumes, particularly Brooks's account of the birth of artistic spirit in the young nation, they condemned him for initiating that attitude toward history which today has apparently become stock-in-trade among our historians of a usable past. Brooks's nineteenth-century New England, Dupee remarked, "purged of conflict and contradiction," is presented as an "idyll of single-hearted effort." What was found unfit for this "fairy-tale" was disposed of.

In the beginning of his career he had sailed over uncharted waters, rediscovered forgotten islands, wrecked ships, lost continents. In the late thirties, however, he wrote history with his eye on that cold black draughty void out of which he had so lately emerged. Our minds are darkest Africas, he told Granville Hicks in 1936, and he was at that moment exploring his own jungle trying to discover what he believed: half the fun of writing a book was in finding out what our souls tell us we must think. Or, as he was to say in his sketch of Helen Keller, "She might have taken as her motto Theodore Roethke's line, 'I learn by going where I have to go.' "

Roethke's line could serve as his motto, surely, but could not justify the results of his explorations either of the history of the writer in America—the subtitle chosen for Makers and Finders—or of his own inner history as an American prophet. For all the wisdom and chic of Roethke's remark, its bearing on Brooks's actual conduct of his own life is miniscule. Brooks's practice as a historian was determined less by the spirit of adventure which marked the first period of his career than by an imperial spirit which signified his sense of conquest during the second period of his life. What he triumphed over—though every morning brought a new test of conquest—was the terror of disintegration which was to torment him from the early thirties until his death.

Celebrating Brooks's courage, Sherman Paul speaks for all those—among whom I list myself—who admire that prodigious man's lifelong allegiance to "the high responsibilities of the literary vocation": in a country where "the writer seldom matures and most often goes down to defeat, he managed to drive on to the end." That Brooks did survive shipwreck and manage to assume once again the responsibilities of his calling must be put down in part to Eleanor Brooks's devotion. That he managed to drive on to the end must be in part an effect of his second marriage, to Gladys Rice Billings. In 1946, following his wife's death Brooks left Westport. It had been a twenty-six-year residence. During the following two years he lived in New York and—though I myself at that time of course knew very little of all this—would appear regularly at Columbia. A five-year gap of publication separates the fourth volume (1947) in his historical series from the fifth (1952). The only work published in the interim was a collection of earlier writings, A *Chilmark Miscellany* (1948), completed at Martha's Vineyard in the summer after his marriage to that remarkable woman with whom he eventually returned to Connecticut, to Bridgewater, where he lived until he died. And there, as is well known, he sat each day twelve hours at his desk, turning out essays, sketches, biographies, composing the final volume of his history. "Work was the great protector," Robert Gorham Davis has said, against despair. For Brooks was never really free of that terror which had so long enveloped him.

Mrs. Gladys Brooks has recently published a memoir, *If Strangers Meet* (1967), which complements Brooks's own recollection of this final stage of his life. In both books her role in helping to lift the shadow is plainly shown. Or as Mr. Davis has said, summarizing Mrs. Brooks's effect on her husband, "she identified herself completely with his life and friendships," and toward the end helped him to sustain an ever-wavering faith. Brooks himself apparently took special pleasure in the sort of life incarnate in Gladys Brooks whom, fittingly, he met in his friend Wheelock's apartment: Wheelock had known Eleanor Brooks when they had both been young. Remarkably, too, Gladys Brooks was the daughter of Mark Twain's doctor, had been David Mannes's earliest violin pupil, subject of a drawing by Sargent, a "niece" of Henry Adams—very much, in sum, an American heroine, heiress of all the ages, participant in an interwoven tapestry of scenes and portraits of the kind Brooks had always especially enjoyed. And above all, as her reminiscence shows, she had been a woman accustomed to act according to lines set down in Roethke's verse.

Both wives and work therefore protected Brooks against the void. Brooks himself maintained, in the books to which we turn now, those written during the last quarter-century of his life, that his early books had simply undervalued the American experience and that his later work merely restored balanced judgment to American studies. This position he staked out in the five volumes of history, the sketches of John Sloan (1955), Helen Keller (1956) and William Dean Howells (1959), the account of American expatriates in Italy, *The Dream of Arcadia* (1958), as well as in the imposing array of works in self-explanation and self-justification: *Opinions of Oliver Allston* (1941), *The Writer in America* (1953), *From a Writer's Notebook* (1958), the three volumes of autobiography published intermittently from 1954 to 1961.

But the heart of the matter involves the interplay of proportion and distortion in Brooks's art. Although all writers must find external forms for internal states, must make their way through a labyrinth of motives, only a few are able to achieve an immersion in and conversion of but not subversion by their deepest wants. Brooks's myth-making embodied his inner life in vastly larger measure than it represented the exterior world, but until 1925 he contrived to transform the urgencies of private need into a prescription for society as a whole. Converting a private refuge into a public preserve, discovering in personal perplexity the key to a national dilemma, he defined some central confusions in American life and found for himself a short-lived relief from neurosis. Thereafter, following the period of psychosis, he duplicated Aschenbach's feat in Mann's story *Death in Venice*: exercising an iron will he held fast to the highest idealisms of the American mind in order to evade submersion within his own Cimmerian abyss. In those late books, said a loyal friend of the *Dial* and the *Freeman* days, Alyse Gregory, it seemed that he wrote largely from habit and desperation, the technique of composition sustaining itself almost of its own volition. It sustained him to the very end, this fusion of maladies and motives, so that Brooks himself, in ways which he could not have foreseen, became the avatar of his own belief. "Whatever turbulence was within—and we know there was often much—" said Roger Burlingame in euology for *The Century Association Yearbook* (1964), "his outward presence suggested serenity, peace of mind, and the constant impulse of giving."

5

The Talismanic Word

> You have laid our literature open to the sunlight and air of common day. Henceforth, much that was seemingly buried forever will be accessible; and much that we thought we knew will be forever different because of what you have revealed of the conditions out of which it grew.—Lewis Mumford, 1940

Makers and Finders, the chief ornament of Brooks's second career, is both a splendid achievement and a pernicious work. "Our greatest sustained work of literary scholarship," Cowley has said, it has also been responsible for that view of the past which claims that authentic American literature avoids extremes, is neither high nor lowbrow but draws its inspiration from a will to heal breach, resolve antithesis, banish contradiction. This view leads to the celebration of a style of literary culture, middlebrow, in which contrarieties are denied. It is a view, too, which bolsters an ideal of social order, in the style of Lyndon B. Johnson or Richard Nixon in which in the name of consensus radical conflict is ignored or suppressed. Above all it is a view which rests not on the history of ideas but on an illusion, a fable. And fables, Descartes said, "make one imagine many events possible which in reality are not so, and even the most accurate of histories, if they do not exactly misrepresent or exaggerate the value of things in order to tender them more worthy of being read, at least omit in them all the circumstances which are basest and least notable."

The key to Brooks's failure as a historian is contained in

a remark addressed to Cowley (October 1939): "For there is an American grain, and I wish to live with it, and I will not live against it knowingly." Adopting William Carlos Williams's phrase, he decided that this figure of speech, taken literally, would enable him to discover exactly what was usable, what was "organic" in the American past. Whatever else must be said of this doctrine, it can be seriously faulted as an unambiguous example of what the medievalist Johan Huizinga called historical anthropomorphism and defined as "the tendency to attribute to an abstract notion behavior and attitudes implying human consciousness." This tendency, he noted, leads all too smoothly to another, to a reliance on the resources of figurative speech, metaphor, personification, allegory. Whenever "historical presentation is fraught with passion, whether political, social, religious," figurative language shades into myth and dispatches all hope of science. And if "beneath the metaphors the claim remains that the figure of speech is still to be taken philosophically and scientifically," then indeed is anthropomorphism a subversive act of the mind.

Although Huizinga in this essay ("Historical Conceptualization," 1934) doubtless intended these reflections to bear on the problem of writing history in that day of ideology, fascist and communist, his thought illumines the problem of Brooks's ideology, too, the ideology of the American grain. Brooks, who was himself alert to the dangers of his position, wrote into the *Opinions of Oliver Allston* a crucial chapter, "A Philosophical Interlude," designed to circumvent judgments of this kind. As figures of authority he chose a heterodox group of system-makers—Croce, Thoreau, William James, Spengler—and drew from each what it suited him to have. Croce it was who led him to understand that America was "idealistic in its grain and essence" and that "the American mind was saturated with a sense of 'that which has to be,'—again in Croce's words, as opposed to 'that which is.'" If this view was considered unscientific, as Brooks anticipated his critics saying, so much the worse for science which is after all a discipline of thought not a guarantor of wisdom. Citing James, Allston remarked that

truly wise men of science, "whenever they offered reflections
on general problems, offered them, not officially as men of
science, but as men who had lived and thought *through the
mode of science*." (Brooks's italics). Besides, he had come
to realize that he could make no "headway with abstract
thinking, and, feeling that life was short he abandoned
himself to his tastes. To justify himself again, he copied out
a passage from Thoreau's Journals (Vol. V): 'It is essential
that a man confine himself to pursuits . . . which lie next
to and conduce to his life, which do not go against the
grain, either of his will or his imagination? . . . Dwell as
near as possible to the channel in which your life flows.' "

Thoreau's view is unexceptionable. But nothing he said
in his journals or anywhere else could justify Brooks's conviction that a peculiar socialismus of art and politics was
apple pie but that "the communist mind runs counter to
the American grain." This assertion occurs in the chapter
on socialism in *Oliver Allston* where Brooks commended
Williams for his fine phrase, then repeated the sentence
from his letter to Cowley, and propelled himself headlong
into the task of devising a whole new vocabulary of terms
generated by the magical word, grain, itself. Creating this
new language, Brooks deliberately excised from his own
discourse the two main forms of talk common among intellectuals of that era, the Formalists' and the Marxists'.
Rejecting both forms of speech as a "private language of
personal friends" which was divorced from "organic bonds
with family life, the community, nature," he imagined that
these bonds would be restored by way of his new terminology.

Many years earler, writing in eulogy of his friend Bourne,
Brooks had said that "every writer possesses in his vocabulary one talismanic word which he repeats again and again,
half-unconsciously, like a sort of signature, and which reveals the essential secret of his personality. In Bourne's case
the word is 'wistful.' " In Brooks's case the word is *grain*:
reified, endowed with independent and objective life, this
talismanic word conferred on Brooks's criticism the authority
of pure American speech. Expanding its range to include an
infinitude of reference, Brooks searched the language of

psychotherapy for endorsement of his formula of praise and blame. Today a debased Freudianism pervades the cant-talk of common parlance but thirty years ago it had not yet suffused standard speech. And Brooks, who had introduced Hart's language into the study of Mark Twain's life, now psyologized the Elioteers. To be always in reaction was "juvenile or adolescent"—were not, therefore, Eliot and Pound and Joyce infantile, sick, immature? "Were they not really unequal to life," these nay-sayers; did they not poison one another with their despair, and poison society too? Had not these very influential men of letters "lost a sense of the distinction between primary literature and coterie literature—was it not time to make this distinction clear?" Like primary instinct, "primary literature somehow follows the biological grain," he said, defining the exact "centre of his thought." Primary literature "favours what psychologists call the 'life-drive.'" The only value of coterie literature was its shock value which, like "insulin treatment for schizophrenia," restores the mind to its primitive state, a state of readiness for the fresh start. But this treatment, coterie literature, is hardly necessary in America where the primary virtues of courage, justice, mercy, honor, and love represent the "tap-root" of art and "the sum of literary wisdom." To live in harmony with the American grain, in short, was to ally oneself with the forces of eros and set oneself in resolute opposition to the forces of thanatos, the vanguard, coterie-writers, "children sucking their thumbs," who incarnate "the 'death-drive' more than the 'life-drive.'"

Oliver Allston is an intemperate work. In private comment Brooks qualified its contentions, allowed that his attack had its faults. And he told Norman Foerster in 1942, the book was intended as a sketch of attitude merely and should have been amplified with pros and cons: he should have differentiated among various groups of modern writers and not given the impression that he opposed them all. But in truth no amount of differentiation could have modulated Allston's tone or moderated his spleen. Furthermore the *Opinions of Oliver Allston* were identical with Brooks's opinions in the first two volumes of his literary history.

Strikingly, too, his opinions helped to confirm an opposition to modern literature in that new audience which read *The Flowering of New England* (1936), and awarded Brooks in 1937 a Pulitzer Prize. No longer addressing himself to the Young Generation of literary men, Brooks became a hero of middle-aged and middlebrowed culture—became, as the *Partisan Review* nastily said, a pilgrim to Philistia. All too comfortably, his former colleagues felt, Brooks slipped into the role of spokesman for a public to which modernist literary forms were impenetrable and modernist ideas were unthinkable. All too easily, many former allies thought, he assumed the role of laureate of American chauvinism. Only Mumford preserved both respect and love in unchanging measure: your literary history establishes a new genre, he wrote Brooks in 1944, and presents its readers with a sort of natural history of the American spirit. But Mary Colum, whose essay two decades earlier had described Brooks as a pathfinder, a contributor of transforming ideas, spoke for nearly everyone else when she told him that nothing he wrote about modern art showed that he knew what he was talking about.*

There was in truth nothing in modern writing that Brooks cared anything for. What he did care about was to flush and dispel once and for all the issue of expatriation. Confessing that in his youth he had been "morbid" about this matter, that he had been "drawn to Europe over-much," that "many years had passed before he had learned to love his country," before he had realized that "he must cling to America to preserve his personality from disintegration"— these extraordinary confessions clarify the reasons for the conversion of Van Wyck Brooks and signify which motives underlay his fable. Along with the first, the remaining four

---

* "Mrs. Colum has the most beautiful red hair I have ever seen and an intelligence as sharp as a butcher's knife," Burton Rascoe, echoing a general opinion, had said in *A Bookman's Daybook* (1929). In a more formal way but with no less asperity, F. R. Leavis in a 1952 essay (reprinted in *Anna Karenina and Other Essays*, 1967) called "The Americanness of American Literature," described Brooks's *Makers and Finders* as "inflationary" in tendency, marked by a blindness and indifference to "real American achievement."

books in the series—*New England: Indian Summer* (1940), *The World of Washington Irving* (1945), *The Times of Melville and Whitman* (1947), *The Confident Years* (1952) —result of nearly twenty years of independent research, supported only now and then by a grant-in-aid, form a national archives of forgotten documents, misplaced books, lost lives. Reading everything he could find lest anything of the least interest be neglected, Brooks restored to general view enormous numbers of hitherto ghostly figures. And if it were possible to set aside the fable, to take these five books as a moveable feast of the American imagination, Makers and Finders would represent an absolute triumph of humane learning. If Brooks had had no larger aim than to revive a sort of racial memory among American readers and writers, there would be universal agreement to Cowley's view: these books caused "a revolutionary change in our judgment of the American past" and a "radical change in our vision of the future."

But it is impossible to set aside either the ideology of the American grain or the allegory of a usable past. How, for example, can we square Brooks's remark in a letter of 1933— "I wish we could have in America the guild-life that writers have in England"—with the remark, made exactly two decades later in the essay "Makers and Finders" in which Brooks set down his final thoughts on his study of American history: "It seemed to me that . . . our writers formed a guild, that they had even worked for a common end." Presumably it was twenty years' research into the usable past which had led him to a major discovery. Reading through the five volumes, however, you are nonplussed trying to retrace the ground of Brooks's discoveries, trying to learn where Brooks had located this guild-life of American writers. Apart from a modest measure of support for this notion in Boston during its heyday, the whole drift of evidence contradicts Brooks's point. Here are some examples taken nearly at random from *The Times of Melville and Whitman:* for nineteen years in New York, Melville was "all but forgotten as a man of letters." And Whitman—"to the end of his life the great magazines excluded him." After the first "flurry of interest on the part of Emerson and the dead Thoreau, he had for years only a handful of readers." Undoubtedly Whitman was "warped" by this treatment, Brooks says. Mark Twain, too, was warped by his conviction that American writers were merely "manacled servants of the public"—as if Walt Whitman "had never existed or Emerson or the free Thoreau or Cooper." Again, speaking of the main patterns of literary life in the seventies and eighties, when a first wave of writers fled America, Brooks quotes Charles Godfrey Leland, whom in an earlier volume he had treated as a man with deep intellectual and emotional ties to his native Philadelphia. "I have nothing to keep me here. There is nothing to engage my ambitions."

Despite contentions made after the fact, Brooks was unable to prove that nineteenth-century American writers had indeed formed a guild. And in time he substituted another theme, one closer to the heart of his passion, easier to illustrate: the replacement of rural life with urban life. "More and more, as the eighties advanced and the cities grew larger and larger, the old life of the farm receded in the national mind." It was to this theme that Brooks committed himself without reserve. Describing the "immemorial rural life," genesis of "the American point of view," he wove arabesques of history which were intended to show how a once "homogeneous people, living close to the soil, intensely religious, unconscious, unexpressed in art and letters, with a strong sense of home and fatherland" was uprooted and dispersed. In the middle of the last century, "one of its towns becomes a 'culture-city,' for Boston . . . answers to this name, which Spengler accords to Florence." There was then a "moment of equipoise, a widespread flowering of the imagination in which the thoughts and feelings of the people . . . find expression. Then gradually the mind, detached from the soil, grows more and more self-conscious. Contradictions arise within it, and worldlier arts supplant the large, free, ingenuous forms through which the poetic mind had taken shape. . . . The Hawthornes yield to the Henry Jameses . . . and the culture-city itself surrenders to the world-city,—Boston surrenders to New York,—which stands for cosmopolitan deracination."

Determined at any cost to display the consistency of these ideas, Brooks engaged in exactly the kind of struggle he had recognized in Symonds, that "congested poet" who, upon recovery from breakdown, had assumed the "fretful activity" of a *vulgariseur* and had set down with great labor large works of scholarship which tried to do what "only poetry can do." He did not know, he told M. A. De Wolfe Howe in 1934, how to use his thousands of notes, but it was increasingly clear to him that he could not think in an expository form. As he proceeded from book to book his vision clarified itself. He would recreate the dream of paradise. And there his fancy fled in order to preserve his mind against disintegration, against any relapse of despair. No matter how far he ranged, this dream remained constant. Facts could not dislodge it though certain non-facts could be introduced to support it—the posthumous papers of Constance Rourke, for example, or the phenomenal fact of Helen Keller's life.

When, therefore, at approximately midpoint in research for Makers and Finders, in 1942, he paused to edit Miss Rourke's studies of American folktale and legend, *The Roots of American Culture and Other Essays,* he discovered in these studies a motif all his own. That this book attests Brooks's high regard for Constance Rourke is unquestionable. That Brooks's views and Miss Rourke's views overlapped is unarguable. For Brooks's preface accurately reports that Miss Rourke "studied American architecture, the early American theatre, early American music, the American novel, Negro folklore, the old Shaker colonies" and assembled proofs of a rich creative life marked by distinctively native elements. But then, shaping these proofs to form some general ideas, Brooks shades Miss Rourke's preoccupations a little and presents her work as indirect testimony vindicating his own views on that loaded and profoundly personal concept, primary literature. It is quite one thing to study the primitive forms of imaginative life in order to discover the origins of national culture and quite another thing to suggest that a special state of grace exists by virtue of that discovery.

Pursuing Brooks through nearly three thousand pages,

entranced by gossip, hypnotized by the shimmer of detail and enthralled by this display of mastery in the stern art of narrative history, we are tempted to celebrate grace. But when we draw together the main lines of belief on which his faith rests—when we realize that one way to take these five volumes, according to Morton and Lucia White's *The Intellectual and the City* (1962), is as "the most striking example of anti-urbanism" in contemporary popular thought —we discover an illusion. I am working in the morning and in the afternoon, exploring the South, he notified Granville Hicks in 1936, and hotly reading the South Carolina writers, at last with some gleams of understanding. When this exploration of South Carolina was made public, in *The World of Washington Irving*, his understanding of that state's contribution to American letters (concentrated in the effects of Charleston on William Gilmore Simms) was identical to his view of the effect of Knickerbocker New York on Irving, Philadelphia on Charles Brockden Brown, of Monticello, Cooperstown, and above all Boston on other literary men of the age.

Having adopted Spengler's idea of "culture cycles"—for which Spengler "has made a case that is so suggestive as to seem conclusive"—Brooks arrived at a definition of the American grain which he must have felt was unassailable. At the point of origin in American civilization, we can now say in paraphrase of his final position on this whole matter, a primary literature develops out of one of the two primary instincts of the unconscious, the life-drive. Serving as the source of high-mindedness in politics, it brought American national experience to fruition, united high art and heroic action, joined the cities and the plains during a century of national life. Then, in manifestation of cyclic laws governing all organisms, in conjunction with the decline of rural life, the death-drive acquired authority. And it in turn generated that coterie literature which accompanied the rise of great urban centers. Made of greed, fruit of thanatos, these deracinated modern cities brought catastrophe to birth out of the world's body. In the last pages of the final volume, winding up the allegory, Brooks's mind resorted once again to its first imagery, the imagery of dualism. Although his joy in dialectic is muted in the first four volumes, the end pages of *The Confident Years* present recent American history as a battleground between the forces of urban and the forces of rural life. A private taste for antithesis in thought is transformed into a vision of apocalypse in which the "life-affirmers" engage in a battle of the books with the "life-deniers." Wherever one "looked, in literature or in life, one found the two contrasting types," fighting it out as Brooks fought it out in unceasing battle with Eliot and the Elioteers.* So deeply engrained in the American mind is life-affirmation, however, that the outcome was never in serious question. Because life-affirmation expresses the ineradicable will of the American spirit, it must eventually bring into being a new primary literature which will save the world from destroying itself. This was the perpetually fresh dream of utopia on which Brooks staked his life.

Is it fair to say of all this, as he himself said of Symonds's achievement, that it was mere "high fantasy"? Had he composed book after book in praise of roots in order to devise for himself an utterly fanciful sanctuary? Is the figure of speech which he chose to describe Amiel and James an apt figure of self-description too: did he surround himself, spiderlike, in a shelter spun from his own body? Had he labored to transform the idea of expatriation, of escape, of flight into so sticky and labyrinthine a version of the American pastoral myth that only the most determined and powerful of Hindus could have found him out?

None of these is a fair question. All propose answers

---

* Most of Brooks's friends sympathized but disagreed with Brooks's views on Eliot. A few years after the appearance of *The Confident Years*, in October 1957, Wilson wrote a marvelous letter to Brooks, more a short essay than a letter, in which he said that he'd been brooding on Eliot since their—Wilson's and Brooks's—conversations, and had decided that in Eliot there were both a scoundrel and an actor. The young man, a young scoundrel, had written the fine poetry and the old man, an old scoundrel, was playing out a public performance. Behind both masks you could discern a shrewd Yankee, a man both cunning and idealistic. Ending these remarks, Wilson implied that he did not think that he could sway Brooks who had always regarded Eliot as a more sinister figure.

which are probably less true than false but are just true enough to record the fact that Brooks's unconscious life played a more intrusive and persuasive role in deciding the course of his career than was good for Brooks or for the history of ideas in our time. No essay in the psychology of motive, however, can deprive Brooks of his role as a leader of the new radicalism in American letters. And because it was in the performance of this role that Brooks first earned and has continued to deserve his fame, that I am at a loss to understand why Christopher Lasch's good book on this subject, *The New Radicalism in America* (1965), takes up Bourne but utterly disregards Brooks. This lapse is the more startling in that Mr. Lasch's account of the radical tradition, very little modified, might stand as a virtual biography of Brooks's mind. At the outset, in 1900, reformers sought to see society from the ground up "or at least from the inside out," Mr. Lasch says. Eventually this new class of intellectuals came to distrust the intellect, "to forsake the role of criticism and to identify themselves with what they imagined to be the laws of historical necessity and the working out of the popular will." Of this movement and process Brooks is indisputably the prime example.

Before he renounced the role of a radical critic, he imposed his stamp on two generations of reformist literary men, on Mumford, Cowley, Waldo Frank, Matthew Josephson, Granville Hicks, Newton Arvin—above all on F. O. Matthiessen whose *American Renaissance* undertook to augment the Brooksian study of myth with the techniques of formal, textual analysis. In this way, Matthiessen believed, American criticism might achieve the repossession of "all the resources of the hidden past in a timeless and heroic present." As Matthiessen took up the subject where Brooks left off, so too others simply adopted certain main themes of Brooks's thought, Hemingway in the *Green Hills of Africa*, for example: "We do not have great writers. . . . Something happens to our good writers at a certain age." In 1935 Hemingway's readers recognized Hemingway's reference. Today Brooks's ideas receive cachet of the most flattering kind in that these are no longer recorded as Brooks's at all but seem to express perennial wisdom. Reading a series of axioms on American literature in the *Times Literary Supplement* (July 20, 1967), we realize that the writer is unaware that he has reproduced a configuration of ideas which goes back fifty years to those first books in which Brooks examined our "impulse toward literary cosmopolitanism" and explored the "springs and sources of art and the right environment for its creation." It is this impulse "which has been of enormous importance in shaping the character of modern literature. Indeed it has been of the greatest importance for western literature generally, since the very idea of modernism seems to have its roots in this cosmopolitan, expatriate spirit." This matter of expatriation and cosmopolitanism has been of presiding importance in modern writing not because some leading American writers have been expatriates but because Brooks, obsessed by the problems of rootedness and deracination, their effect on the creative life in Europe and America, engaged in a single-handed and single-minded attempt to disclose the genesis of literature and discover the right environment for its creation. Although he turned out to be a critic of divided mind, a man whose life was broken in half, in one key respect his career was all of a piece: from first to last he sought to transform America from an industrial jungle into a cosmopolitan place, fit for the realization of Emerson's romantic dream.

This vast realm was once his private preserve. At the point when he turned his mind toward other problems, when the state of affairs within his own mind became a most troublesome problem, his friends tried to recall him to himself. "Do not, we beg you," Edmund Wilson addressed him in 1924, "lose too much the sense of that wonder," that excitement of the artist "enchanted by the spectacle of life." It was both good advice and bad. And in any event it came too late. For Brooks was already disabled by some critical side effects of what the English writer Tony Tanner has called the reign of wonder in classic American letters. Mr. Tanner talks round Brooks but frames the general issue in ways which correlate his life with the lives of those great men of the nineteenth century, Emerson and Whitman and Mark Twain, who loom so large in Brooks's imagination. Like them, he was "too suspicious of analytical intellect, too disinclined to develop a complex reaction to society, too much given to extreme reactions, too hungry for meta-physics" to avoid what Brooks himself had recognized as an American malady, the malady of the Idea.

Surely it is time to install Brooks among his predecessors and peers, those American romantics who have traditionally yearned to experience and to portray the "wholeness of the universe." It is time, too, to save him from entombment in the American Academy of Arts and Letters and from en-shrinement as Bishop of Bridgewater, Connecticut. For if it is just the effigy of a former oracle that is preserved, then the legend of Van Wyck Brooks will in the end turn out to be simply routine and we too will have assisted at this waste of history. But because no man ever wanted less for himself, as Bernard Smith remarked thirty years ago, and more for his fellow men, the time has come to restore Brooks to the highest place among the most eminent of twentieth-century literary intellectuals in America, those celebrants of con-science in whom the idea of America served both as a cause of malady and as a genesis of motive. "My 90th birthday was a surprising occasion. Friends wanted to celebrate it," said W. E. B. DuBois, but were hard put in 1958 to find sponsors. Among the few who appeared at the dedication of William Zorach's bust of DuBois in the New York Public Library, "Van Wyck Brooks took part."

Convinced though I am of Brooks's honor I cannot end my essay on so pious a note. Its tone is wrong, unsuited to the kind of book I have hoped to write. For Brooks is no legendary hero of American writing who must be once more restored to fashion, nor is he a clay idol, who must be finally cast out. And if it is true that he was in very large degree a selfless servant of his cause, it is also true that his ideas very often served to screen, from himself and his public, deep-seated and very personal passions: he adopted the cause of messianism in order to save himself from disin-tegration. For it required a lifetime's labor to establish and maintain a truce between the thrust and counterthrust of his ambition and temper. An expatriate, he decided that submission to an American fate was the price of peace. A pacifist, he broke with his friends in order to support the First World War. A socialist who believed in "a socialized world and a socialized country," he sentimentalized the American farmer. An antitotalitarian who in 1939 refused to support the League of American Writers because it did not oppose Stalin's dictatorship as staunchly as it opposed Hitler's, he would have welcomed the sight of Eliot behind barbed wire. As a pacifist, socialist, utopist, therefore, he somehow evaded the final consequences of his belief. And as a critic of literature, he invented a complicated metaphysics with which he hoped to justify his inability, a sheerly emotional incapacity to anchor his thought in the firm and convincing ground of textual analysis and debate. Thereby he lost the favor of those to whom he owed his fame—of James Sibley Watson, Jr., for example, publisher of the *Dial*: "Brooks says that Margaret Fuller was a more significant critic than Poe because she was 'less interested in the technical aspect of literature and more in its spirit.' The distinction is suspicious; the word 'spirit' more so. And Brooks has gone Margaret Fuller one better by criticizing modern literature without naming work and author. It is all spirit for him." Watson, whose pseudonym was W. C. Blum, backed W. C. Williams's version of the American grain, not Van Wyck Brooks's.

But in Margaret Fuller and the transcendentalists, in Van Wyck Brooks and his school of evangels, we discover a peculiarly national style to which Continental or English intellectuals—René Wellek, Tony Tanner—are immeasurably more sympathetic than Americans are. And it is their judgment, drawn in this final instance from the *Times Literary Supplement* (November 9, 1967), with which I end this essay on the most ingenious, persistent, influential contributor to the prophetic tradition in contemporary American life and thought.

But among the few genuine types that America has contributed to the repertoire of feeling that of . . . the lofty or ribald annunciator of values—moral, national, cosmic—does stand out. We find it at precisely those places in which the diverse strains of the American tone, the puritanical and the lyric-prophetic, the homely and the crass, crystallize. It helps define Emerson and H. L. Mencken, Will Rogers and Thoreau. It is as crucial to the high flights of Walt Whitman as to the lapses of Mark Twain . . . it animates the public intimacies and histrionic clairvoyance of Paul Goodman and Norman Mailer. Watcher at the gate . . . vatic bard or television humorist—there is a distinctive brand of American writers and "talkers" who carry on the tradition of the frontier publicist travelling the wide land with . . . shreds of apocalypse and nostrums for spirit and bowels.

Mr. Lewis Mumford is very much of that tribe.

So he is—the last Orphic voice of the twenties generation, as Brooks was in his time the first.

Appendixes

The following pages present a series of essays by Van Wyck Brooks, written mainly during the final years of Brooks's life, 1960–63, works both ambitious and modest in scope. Each was written for a particular occasion or in response to a specific invitation. And most served as prefaces to a series of reprints of illustrious but half-forgotten works to which Brooks sought to restore a lost lustre. A number of these prefaces—chiefly those treating books whose lure survives more or less undiminished—are more accurately described as essays in appreciation than essays in criticism, for Brooks apparently relied on appreciation when he found himself unable to enlarge or improve on earlier writings. But even these are worth preserving. Taken together with older critical pieces, the whole group presents all Brooks's virtues and recalls to our attention a critic adroit in the uses of large learning, venturesome in the exercise of taste, shrewd and elegant in sensibility. In the final years, when a diminished vitality is at all noticeable, it shows itself more in the tone of Brooks's voice than in the quality of Brooks's thought.

A main result of his last enterprise—and a striking effect of this collection—is our rediscovery of a coherent oeuvre on American realism. In itself this is a matter worth remarking and attending. And even more remarkable is the method to which Brooks returned in the end. For this last oeuvre exhibits strong traces of his first style, his deepest vein, his fascination with the radical connections which link a writer's personality and art. And this was indeed, as Edmund Wilson told him in a letter of the 1950s, the special mark of his genius. Another and more obvious result of this last collection of Brooks's work, as Brooks himself observed of Chiang

Yee's *The Silent Traveller in New York,* is its power to kindle appreciation and dilate understanding. However arguable the question of Brooks's full attainment, it is surely unarguable that he was bountifully endowed with this enlivening gift.

A final word: I know of only two other items by Brooks which are not generally available, "Commemorative Tributes" to Sinclair Lewis and to Willa Cather delivered by Brooks at the American Academy of Arts and Letters and published by the Academy in 1951.

Introduction to
The Sketch Book of Geoffrey Crayon, Gent.

When Washington Irving arrived in England, on the voyage he described in the *Sketch Book*, the first news he heard was that Napoleon had fallen. The year was 1815, the battle of Waterloo had been won and England had been rescued from the perils that were bred by this French wolf abroad in the night, a situation that proved propitious for the romantic pilgrim who was to celebrate the old ways of the land of his fathers. For the English, able to breathe freely again, were glad to be reminded of the hearty ancient customs and the relics of the past they had more or less forgotten in the stress of the present, customs and relics that were all the more precious to a transatlantic visitor because so much in his own country was raw and new. Irving was the first of a line of Americans who were fond of the old and the obsolete in proportion as they were starved for these at home, and who, in the mother country of their ancestral culture, looked not so much for what *was* as for what *had been.* He illustrated perfectly the "Toryism of Travellers" of which a later American essayist wrote, and which makes them, eager as they may be to improve conditions at home, the temperamental enemies of progress and the future elsewhere.

Coming from a country that was full of youthful promise,

Washington Irving was entirely engrossed in the past, and this gave him his great popularity on both sides of the ocean. He could have said nothing of the present of England that would have interested anybody, while, as for America, he was unique in finding antiquity there as well and making his own country a land of myths and legends. He possessed what Melville called "the art of old-age-ifying youth in books," endowing with a storied past that was founded in truth and mythology the supposedly prosaic region of the Hudson and New York. By giving it the color of romance and tradition, humanizing the native scene, he added to the pleasure of Americans in their own surroundings, and at the same time the "cultured lag" of the colonial mind rather endeared him than otherwise to readers in England. For he wrote of the English past with both ardor and charm, and this made up for the handicap that his essays were "literary anachronisms," as Hazlitt remarked soon after the *Sketch Book* appeared. Irving, politically at home with the recently established American republic, was, like most Americans of those earlier years, and even like many Americans a century later, still a man of the old country in his imagination, born and brought up, like all colonials, in the cultural air of an earlier day, of an England that the English had long outgrown. For the cultivated circles of Irving's New York Dr. Johnson had never died, and even the days of Queen Anne were not too remote, so it was natural enough that Goldsmith was Irving's favorite author and that his first writings savored of Addison and Steele. What might have seemed musty in England was still fresh in New York.

Yet, far from boring British readers, Irving pleased some of the best, among them Sir Walter Scott and Byron, as he pleased all the best at home, becoming a model for many young writers, including the New England romancer Nathaniel Hawthorne. This was in part because, aside from his winning personal note, he was in other respects a man of his own time, a time that was marked, in both writing and painting, by a new feeling for the picturesque that Irving himself possessed in a high degree. An amateur artist, using the pen name "Geoffrey Crayon," Irving had many painters among his friends, and especially the American painter who lived in England, the author of the *Life of Constable*, Charles R. Leslie. He traveled with Leslie, who illustrated Irving's book and painted the sort of scenes that Irving was describing, scenes that were to win the world in the great paintings of Constable and that were often Turneresque. Irving too loved vine-clad mills, village churches with clustering trees, moldering ruins overrun with ivy, all of which he had known well in picture books in childhood and which appealed to the "antiquity hunter" in him. Now also he saw as pictures the stagecoach at Christmas time, the coachman with holiday greens stuck in his coat, the old English Christmas at the country house, the Yule log and the wassail bowl, the hall hung with mistletoe and holly; and it was the special pictorial feeling with which he recorded all these scenes that stamped them not only on the mind but also on the eye. Washington Irving's England was to live on for many years in Christmas cards, posters and illustrations. Generations of children all over the world were to see the "old England" that Irving saw, and as he saw it, because he had seen it first.

So, for all that is threadbare or commonplace in it, the *Sketch Book*, in part at least, was long to retain its element of magic, faint perhaps in the English essays but marked in *Rip van Winkle* and the scarcely less excellent *Legend of Sleepy Hollow*. Goethe, who had read the book and obviously liked these pieces best, remarked in his diary that Irving had made a mistake in neglecting American themes for European, and for this reason he preferred Fenimore Cooper and his stories of American woodsmen, sailors, and scouts. But Irving's talent was not creative in Fenimore Cooper's fashion, nor was he drawn to the primitive scenes and types that fascinated the author of *The Last of the Mohicans*. His nature was ruminative, fanciful, scholarly and bookish, and, as a born traveler and antiquarian, he liked to retell in his own way, with his own additions and ornaments, the tales of others. Not easily at home in the native world in which Cooper and Audubon throve, although later he explored the West and wrote about it, he was drawn to the old countries where stories and legends abounded. In time, developing another phase, Irving became a historian whose work for many years was concerned with Spain, and finally, returning to a New York that was proud of the "father of American letters," he slipped back cheerfully into the world in which he was born. Like Izaak Walton, whom he described as a "mild, sweet, peaceable spirit," he took life as it came, stage by stage, even regarding the feelings of the fishes as the great Angler never did, and accepting the race of critics as "gentle and good-natured." Yet Irving was never namby-pamby, nor was his writing insipid; and for several decades the *Sketch Book* was used as a first reader and a model of prose for students of English in Japan and other countries.

In one of the stories and one of the poems that Melville wrote towards the end of his life he referred with respect and affection to this predecessor as one of those "mellowing immortals," who are both "excellent in their works" and "pleasant and love-worthy in their lives." A literary child of grace, a civilizing influence when America was at the height of its awkward age, Irving was influential too in mending the broken parts of an English-speaking world that had been torn asunder. For the rest, while immortal is too grand a word for this unpretentious writer, he will be remembered as the first in his time and place.

Melville called him

> *happiest Irving*
> *Never from genial verity swerving,*

and the phrase holds good at a later day when many are still drawn by the glow of this sympathetic man of letters.

Introduction to *The Last of the Mohicans*

The forest as Fenimore Cooper had known it from early boyhood is the setting of *The Last of the Mohicans*. Growing up in Cooperstown, New York, a child of the frontier, he had heard wolves and panthers wailing and howling on winter nights; and Lake Otsego, near by, which he called "Glimmerglass," represented for him the grandeur of the woods. There, on Otsego Rock, where Indian tribes resorted for counsel, Hawkeye and Chingachgook had met as young men, and the white scout and his Indian friend of *The Last of the Mohicans* had been intimate companions ever since. Feeling that the Delawares were a scandalized and wronged tribe, Hawkeye had always taken their side; and the two had fought together on Lake Ontario and Lake George when Hawkeye was a scout for the English in their battles with the French. Together they had hunted for the English army, providing it with beavers' tails, venison, and trout.

The Last of the Mohicans is a story of the French and Indian War, written in 1825, the fifth of Fenimore Cooper's novels, and perhaps the best, a tale of flight, pursuit and continuous action. The two daughters, Cora and Alice, of the veteran Scotsman Munro, who is in command of Fort William Henry, travel through the woods in the company of Heyward and of Hawkeye, Chingachgook and his son Uncas. For comic relief they are accompanied by David Gamut, the

Introduction by Van Wyck Brooks, reprinted by permission of the Macmillan Company from *The Last of the Mohicans* by James Fenimore Cooper. © The Crowell-Collier Publishing Company, 1962.

master of psalmody who has come from New England, and they are savagely pursued by Magua and his followers, the Indians who side with the French and the Marquis Montcalm. Heyward, the young officer, is in love with Alice and, in the end, wins her with her father's consent, while the dark-haired Cora, beloved by Uncas, dies with her red lover —the "last of the Mohicans."

Cooper was thirty-seven when he wrote this most popular of all his books, the second of the Leatherstocking series, so called from one of the names of Hawkeye—properly Natty Bumppo—who bears other names in other novels. The Pathfinder, the Deerslayer, the Leatherstocking of *The Pioneers*, a tall gaunt hunter with a foxskin cap, is really the principal character of *The Last of the Mohicans*, a symbol of the primitive forest life. He may have been suggested by a plain old woodsman whom Cooper had seen in Cooperstown, the hamlet in upper New York state that his father had founded, but in any case Hawkeye, with his hunting shirt of forest green, was to live as one of the great characters of fiction. His gravity and piety, his sinews that never tired, his silent and peculiar way of laughing, his sturdy nature and single mind, acute, cool, and daring, made him the perfect scout of the American forest. The Indian Chingachgook's lifelong friend, quick, simple and sagacious, he had never seen the sun except through the trees and, able to walk fifty miles without stopping, he had never experienced either fatigue or weakness. His fatherly care of the young girls went with the love of justice that made him unwilling to say that he hated all his enemies, and he buried these when he found them dead, not liking to have creatures of his own kind bleaching in the rain. What he disliked above all was the "din" of the settlements, as he loved the beauty of the woods. A link between the Indians and civilized life, he knew the difference between the prints of an Indian's foot and the foot of a white man, and he never crossed a rivulet without attentively considering the quantity, the speed and the color of the water. He could see the edging of blackness on the lower side of a cloud indicating a fire that had been suffered to burn low; and, little as he liked the spilling of blood, there was not a square mile around Lake George on which his long rifle "Killdeer" had not dropped a body.

This was the region that Cooper said was as little known as the steppes of Tartary or the deserts of Arabia. But he had always known it. As a midshipman in the navy he had walked to Lake Ontario, where the brig *Oneida* was being constructed, observing this wild frontier, spending his nights in the woods, listening to the moaning sounds that arose from the forest. He knew the rippling of watercourses, and he knew the importance of hiding his trail by traveling in the dry bed of a stream. He knew all the New York lakes, Oneida, Seneca, Lake Champlain, but for him, as for Hawk-eye, Lake George, the old French *Lac du Saint Sacrement*, was by far the loveliest of all. He compared Lake George with the Swiss and Italian lakes which it equaled, he said, in outline and purity of water. It was superior in the number of its isles and islets. Wherever he went he had a passion for landscape, and Balzac called one of his novels "the school of study for literary landscape-painters."

Cooper knew American history as he knew natural scenery. He had picked up in the woods, near the ruins of Fort Oswego, decayed old scaling-ladders that had been lying since 1776. He knew survivors of the Revolution, Lafayette, and John Jay, to whom he had read the manuscript of his first novel and who had told him the story he had used in *The Spy*, a story in which George Washington appeared as a character. He certainly knew the Indians too, from the Oneidas he had seen as a boy, camping in the woods near Cooperstown, to the deputations of Western tribes that visited cities in the East and whom he had followed once to Washington. He had had a long talk with a Pawnee chief, grave, courteous, and dignified; he visited many tribes in the state of New York; and, while most of the Indians in his novels are merciless and crafty, he greatly admired some of the types he met. Their firm and upright attitudes, their erectness and agility appealed to Cooper as they appealed to others who knew the Indians best, Schoolcraft, George Catlin the painter who lived with them, David Crockett, and the poet Whitman later. Hawkeye said that to Indian eyes a hummingbird left its trail in the air, and, as Cooper saw, their poetical images were based upon the clouds, the seasons, the birds, the beasts, the vegetable world. He said their oratory was Oriental and that the Indians had probably brought it with them from the other continent. It was a link connecting the ancient histories of America and Asia.

The Last of the Mohicans was written near Scarsdale, New York, where Cooper with his wife lived for a while. He had resigned from the navy, after serving for nearly four years, though it gave him scenes and subjects for a dozen sea tales. Many of the young men in his other novels followed the sea, Mark Woolston and Miles Wallingford, for two examples. He had invented the sea novel in his long story *The Pilot*, the hero of which was John Paul Jones, the first book to picture in detail the movement and handling of vessels. With a passion for the sea that equaled his passion for the woods, he sailed a whaler from Sag Harbor up the Sound to Newport, he kept his own sloop in the Hudson and later he rigged a skiff on Lake Otsego. In Italy, where he spent two years of the seven he passed in Europe, he had his felucca and sailed it to Naples. He went abroad in 1826 and lived in France, Italy, Germany, and Switzerland, famous in all these countries as the first writer about fresh ground and as an American rival of Sir Walter Scott. Cooper's success was prodigious, in fact; he was read even by peasants, and his novels were translated and published in thirty-four cities of Europe, in the Scandinavian countries, in Persia, in Turkey. He found that his name was known in post offices and customhouses, and even at times in country inns; and castles were placed at his disposal while his books were praised by several of the great novelists and critics of Europe.

Cooper returned to America in the years when Andrew Jackson had brought in a kind of democracy that was new in this country, when the gentry had lost their political power and old-fashioned people thought the nation was going to the dogs. There seemed to be a decline in taste and manners, and Cooper, who was distressed by many of these changes, compared the unripeness of America with the ripeness of Europe. He was disgusted with the scramble for money and the general self-complacency, and, loving the country as always, he did not like the way it was going and frankly said so on all occasions. He disliked the rising power of business and the "gulpers" in dining rooms, and, politically minded, he was involved in constant lawsuits, becoming, as Horace Greeley said, censorious and captious. Many of his later books condemned the American ways that he found least to his liking, but Cooper's "open, frank, generous nature," as Horatio Greenough called it, his warm blood and stout heart carried him through to the end.

He had lived for a while in New York but soon returned to Cooperstown, where he spent the last years in his house, Otsego Hall. His friend S. F. B. Morse, the inventor of the telegraph, remodeled it and gave it a castellated roof. There, in his father's time, Talleyrand had spent several days, and a French ex-governor of Martinique had been the village grocer. Thence Cooper had gone to school at Albany with Van Rensselaers, Jays, and Livingstons, and, entering Yale at thirteen, he was expelled at fifteen for a misdemeanor and went off to sea for several years. There, in his older age, at the mouth of the Susquehanna, he returned to the gardening and farming of the years when he had begun to write; and there he produced the books of travel that recorded his life abroad and his pleasure in the scenery of Europe. He turned out novel after novel, indifferent, bad, and good, with a juvenile relish for action as a storyteller, and there he wrote two more novels of the Leatherstocking series that brought back his favorite Natty Bumppo. He could never forget this hero of *The Last of the Mohicans*, stoical, earnest and simple, loyal and just, practiced in the arts of the wilderness as Cooper himself had been in the silence and retirement of the forest. A rough-and-ready writer he was Alexander Dumas' "perpetual delight" and one who, as Joseph Conrad said, "wrote as well as any novelist of his time." All the lesser faults of style of this massive character were lost under his art of storytelling, and *The Last of the Mohicans* shows us how and why.

Introduction to *Uncle Tom's Cabin*

Scarcely any other book in literary history has met with the acclaim that greeted *Uncle Tom's Cabin* in 1852. At home, in America, the dynamic power of the story made it impossible to enforce the Fugitive Slave Law; and a few years later, when the Civil War broke out partly over the question of emancipation, President Lincoln addressed Mrs. Stowe in Washington with the words: "So you're the little woman who made this great war." Mrs. Stowe was compared, by competent critics, with Cervantes and Fielding, and *Uncle Tom's Cabin* was reviewed by Macaulay, George Sand, and Heine whom the book had led to reread the Bible. Three newspapers in Paris published it simultaneously; eighteen publishing houses in London published forty editions of it; the book was translated into thirty-seven languages, and three times into Welsh; while Tolstoy took it, with Dostoyevsky's *House of the Dead*, as a novel of the highest type. In England a petition in twenty-six folio volumes with the signatures of half a million women, praying for the abolition of slavery, was presented to Mrs. Stowe, and Uncle Tom's Cabins rose all over Europe as restaurants, creameries, and bazaars.

Harriet Beecher Stowe herself, the author of many other books, could not account for the intensity with which she

Introduction by Van Wyck Brooks to the Everyman's Library Edition of *Uncle Tom's Cabin* by Harriet Beecher Stowe. Copyright © 1961 by J. M. Dent & Sons, Ltd. Reprinted by permission of E. P. Dutton & Co., Inc.

wrote this one; and in her confused old age, feeling she had been moved by an unknown power, she said one day: "God wrote it." The timing of the book was providential. A few years before England had emancipated the slaves in Jamaica, Russia was on the point of freeing the serfs, and the passing of the Fugitive Slave Law in 1850 brought to a head the question of slavery in the United States. At that time Mrs. Stowe was living in Brunswick, Maine, where her husband was teaching at Bowdoin College, and, as reports of the operation of the law reached her from Boston, she set to work furiously studying the subject. Agents of slavery were hunting out strayed human property, breaking up households, separating husbands, wives, and children and re-enslaving men and women who had long since escaped and in some cases had known as much as ten years of freedom. Mrs. Stowe knew that children were bred to be sold like cattle and she herself had seen a married couple torn apart by a slave trader on an Ohio river wharf. She went herself to Boston to study the lives of escaped slaves in the anti-slavery headquarters there and, reading of a woman who had fled with her child over the broken ice of the Ohio river, she remembered the great blocks of ice tumbling against one another, in spring thaws, when she had lived in Cincinnati. Then, recalling her father's prayers for "poor oppressed, bleeding Africa," she had set out to write the book, under the evening lamp, surrounded by children working over their lessons; for she could write anywhere, on the kitchen table or in the nursery while her babies were being washed and dressed. "Thought, intense, emotional thought, has been my disease," she said; but she could never remember just how or just when she had begun to think of the subject.

Born at Litchfield in Connecticut in 1811, she was the daughter of the well-known minister Lyman Beecher, and, while all her six brothers were to become ministers, she was to marry one herself, "rich in Greek and Hebrew, Latin and Arabic, and alas! in nothing else." As a girl, berry-picking, gathering nuts, and sledding in winter, she had translated Ovid into English verse; and when she heard of Byron's death in the swamps of Missolonghi she lay down among the daisies, according to her own account, looked up at the blue sky and wondered about Byron's soul. All the Beechers had been fascinated by the intensity of Byron's feeling, and Lyman Beecher, aware of his Calvinistic inheritance, had preached a funeral sermon on the poet's death. Harriet, forbidden to read him, had found *The Corsair* and was entranced by the magic of the Byron legend. Meanwhile, brought up on the motto "What hard good work have I to do today?" she became a teacher in her sister's school at Hartford, studying for herself Italian and French and taking lessons from a painting and drawing master. Then at twenty-one she had gone to Cincinnati where her father had become the head of the Lane Seminary. Lyman Beecher had preached revival sermons all the way, and Harriet wrote a tract called *Earthly Care a Heavenly Discipline*. In Cincinnati she met her husband Calvin Stowe, who always "saw things through a glass darkly": he was, in fact, one of Harriet's earthly cares. In her noisy, busy household, after she had married him, cutting out dresses for the children, sweeping and dusting, she had begun to write little pieces for the Western annuals, all about the New England she had left behind. These tales and sketches were sometimes suggested by her husband's reminiscences of the Massachusetts village where he had grown up. Later they formed the basis of her *Old Town Folks*, published in 1869.

In Cincinnati she had her first taste of slavery, for the slave state of Kentucky lay across the river from Ohio; and it was the impressions she had received there that came back to her when she moved to Maine. She crossed the river once or twice to visit a plantation that she was to describe as Colonel Shelby's, a negligent, spacious, opulent place where the Negroes seemed to be carefree in their long cabins covered with vines and set about with patches of garden. The mistress was of "that natural magnanimity and generosity of mind" that Mrs. Stowe always associated with Kentucky women, but she herself could not forget that the slaves were property to be disposed of in case the planter fell into debt. They were likely, as often as not, to be sold down the river to the cotton fields of the deep South, and Mrs. Stowe's cook, brought up

in Virginia as a nurse and seamstress, had been sold into
brutalizing labor in Louisiana. Besides, there were many
gifted Negroes and Mrs. Stowe knew of a man, hired out to
a bagging factory, who had invented a machine for cleaning
hemp. He became, in her story, the husband of Eliza who
escaped with her child to Canada. The "underground railroad," which helped slaves to escape, ran, she wrote, through
her house in Cincinnati; and she remembered that once her
family had slept with a large bell to call the students from
the seminary in case a mob came from the city to search the
house. In *Uncle Tom's Cabin* she did her best to exhibit
slavery as a "living dramatic reality," but she observed: "Who
shall say what yet remains untold in the valley and shadow
of death" she could not reach?

In *A Key to Uncle Tom's Cabin* Mrs. Stowe later assembled the facts, anecdotes and documents on which the story
was founded, a sad but undeniable corroboration of the
darker aspects of the tale. She wrote several other books,
mostly about New England, and in *The True Story of Lady
Byron's Life* she revealed the secret that Byron's wife had
told her in England. It concerned Byron's scandalous relations with his half-sister. Knowing Lady Byron, she had been
outraged by the defense in *Blackwood's* of the Countess
Guiccioli, justifying Byron's mistress and denouncing his
wife as a destructive "moral Clytemnestra." On this second
occasion Mrs. Stowe stirred up a literary hurricane, but it
was not for this that crowds watched for her at railway
stations and hymns were composed in her honor. Almost a
century after the question of slavery had been settled, *Uncle
Tom's Cabin* remained a readable and even exciting book, a
true panorama of American society, fair to the South as well
as the North, generous and humane in its feeling and its
portraiture. It even foresaw the Africa of our day with
republics growing there "with the rapidity of tropical vegeta-
tion." Speaking of the founding of Liberia, Mrs. Stowe said:
"In these days a nation is born in a day. . . . Let us, then,
all take hold together with all our might, and see what we
can do with this new enterprise, and the whole splendid
continent of Africa opens before us," springing up in the

"mighty republics" there. In the optimistic fervor of a hundred years ago, that was a rather good guess; and Uncle Tom and Eliza would have been surprised if they had witnessed the prospect a century later.

Introduction to *Democracy*

Henry Adams was living in Washington when he wrote *Democracy*. The novel was published in 1880, but as early as 1868 Adams had been in the national capital as a "special correspondent," entirely out of sympathy with the Reconstruction political scene and writing articles exposing its corruption. He went back to Boston to teach history at Harvard and edit the *North American Review;* then, returning to Washington as "stable-companion to statesmen," he lived there until he died in 1918. An eager observer of politics, he ceased to write about it and spent several years composing his *History of the United States During the Administrations of Jefferson and Madison.* This was ultimately published in nine volumes. When his wife died in 1885 by her own hand, Adams set forth on travels that took him to Japan and the South Seas. His great books, *The Education of Henry Adams* and *Mont-Saint-Michel and Chartres,* were written in his old age in Washington and Paris.

At the time when he wrote *Democracy,* Adams was surrounded with a congenial circle of Washington friends, especially the John Hays and Clarence King who were called —or called themselves—with Adams and his wife, the "Five of Hearts." The novel, published anonymously, was attributed for many years to both John Hay and Clarence King,

Introduction by Van Wyck Brooks to *Democracy* by Henry Adams. Copyright © 1961, Fawcett Publications, Inc., and reprinted by permission of Fawcett Publications.

and the official announcement that Adams had written it was not made by the publisher until after his death. It was a sensational success. Gladstone, the British Prime Minister, advised people to read it; and Mrs. Humphry Ward said in a review that everyone in England was talking about it, partly because of the unflattering picture it gave of democracy and partly because it seemed to reflect on the United States. It was brought out in unauthorized versions, and Henry Adams himself said, "The wholesale piracy of *Democracy* was the single real triumph of my life." But, if people had associated Adams with novel-writing, they would have seen at once that only he could have written it, for it presented the political scene of the Reconstruction time as he had presented it in his earlier essays.

The novel itself was written in a witty and even brilliant style, somewhat suggesting the early Henry James, and the character of Madeleine Lee was drawn from both the Adamses, partly from Adams himself and partly from his wife. Many of the other characters were suggested by actual persons, just as they were in Adams' later novel, *Esther*, which contained fictionalized portraits of many of his friends. "Old Granite," in *Democracy*, is supposed to have been President Hayes, and Nathan Gore represents John Lothrop Motley, whom President Grant disliked because "he parted his hair in the middle." The figure of Senator Ratcliffe was based on James G. Blaine, who was involved in the Mulligan letters scandal. Madeleine Lee believes that if she marries Ratcliffe she can reform both him and the politics of Washington. But when she questions Ratcliffe about graft, he admits to the same standards he adopted in ordering falsification of election returns to win the Presidency for his party, and save the Union. Madeleine, thereupon, runs away in disgust to Europe, as Henry Adams himself had done to seek a "moral bath" after a year of Grant's administration. Nevertheless, behind all the corruption, was there not a note of hope in Adams's picture of the national capital? — "Underneath the scum floating on the surface of politics, Madeleine felt that there was a sort of healthy ocean current of honest purpose which swept the scum before it and kept the mass pure." At least on one later occasion, Henry Adams himself showed that he was not without hope for the republic. When Owen Wister objected to his scathing remarks about it, he crossed the room, and, laying his hand on Wister's shoulder, said, "Keep the faith!"

Henry Adams had grown up with politics in his blood. As a little boy, he had read Scott and Dickens lying on a pile of Congressional documents in the family house at Quincy. He had been bred in the tradition of the early years of the United States, and for his grandfather and great-grandfather, the two Adams Presidents, public office had been a public trust. These large-minded men had stood for a stable currency, a conservative fiscal policy, and an honest civil service, and Adams had first gone to Washington in 1868 with the belief that he could foster these. Though he felt that he had been born to rule, he knew it could not be in the White House, but he was convinced that he and his friends were to guide the country, as thinkers and critics, through the press. Before he wrote *Democracy*, he had written the life of Albert Gallatin, a statesman of the older dispensation, and the years he spent over this threw into glaring relief the chaos of the post–Civil War time. He learned, just as Mrs. Lee discovered, that in the prevailing anarchy all the old traditions had gone by the board: wildcat finance had replaced a stable policy and government by "deals" had supplanted government by principle. Practical politics, with their ignoble demands, had become the rule in the national capital, and Adams's point of view was permanently altered by this discovery. The central idea of his history was the incapacity of the individual either to control his own destiny or to shape the course of events. This was the "secret of the great American mystery of democracy and government" which Madeleine Lee had set out to discover.

Democracy, in short, was a parable of what Brooks Adams called "the degradation of the democratic dogma." Both—in fact, all—of the Adams brothers had similar ideas regarding the direction, or lack of direction, of American history. But Henry Adams alone had the wit to express these ideas in the form of a scintillating novel.

Introduction to *Their Wedding Journey*

William Dean Howells was thirty-five years old when he published his first novel, *Their Wedding Journey*. In this he mingled travel and fiction and made a story out of his own life. "I was a traveller before I was a noveler," Howells wrote in later years, "and I had mounted somewhat timidly to the threshold of fiction from the high-roads, and by-roads where I had studied manners and men." As consul in Venice during the Civil War years, he had written *Venetian Life* and *Italian Journeys*, and the Venetian playwright Goldoni had taught him how to look at people with his own eyes and not as others saw them. He had been riding a "very high aesthetic horse" during the first of his four years in Venice, and Goldoni led him to forsake the romantic outlook and turned him into the realist that he remained. *Their Wedding Journey* was based on a summer vacation he spent with his wife after he had returned to America in 1865. The Howellses had gone from Boston to New York, to Albany by the night-boat, to Niagara and then to Quebec by the Saint Lawrence. The story that he wove from this was a case in point of what he called "the ante-natal phantom, pleading to be born into the world, the American novel."

For, along with three other short novels he published in the eighteen-seventies, all of which contained a background of travel, Howells was attempting something new in *Their*

Introduction by Van Wyck Brooks to *Their Wedding Journey* by Willian Dean Howells. Copyright © 1960, Fawcett Publications, Inc., and reprinted by permission of Fawcett Publications.

Wedding Journey, a realistic portrayal of American life. Gone were the "females" of Fenimore Cooper, the types of Mrs. Stowe and even the somewhat romanticized characters of Hawthorne, and here in clear actuality appeared people whom all Americans knew, speaking with their proper accents and carefully studied. Howells had seen that, if he was going to do anything worthwhile, he would have to get into fiction from life the things that had not been got into fiction before, and, at a time when we were still "literary colonists . . . beginning to observe the aspects of our own life," he realized for the first time many of these aspects, scenes, types of character, contrasts of section and setting. This novel described the wedding journey of a newly married couple in the days when a visit to Niagara was apart of every honeymoon, when the moon itself was of "lucent honey from the first of June to the last of October" and the country seemed a larger Arcady. In the foreground of every American landscape one saw a bride and groom, and the brides were all charmingly dressed, with ravishing toilets. How small their gloves were, how high the heels of their little boots, over which the snowy skirts electrically fluttered. Basil and Isabel March were a typical bridal pair, not least in their wish not to be taken for one.

Howells's style was the opposite of "all that is Trollopian," for, although he thought better of Trollope later, he was in reaction against "the bad school we were all brought up in." By this he meant the English novel and "the heavy and awkward traditions of the craft" that Dickens and George Eliot perpetuated, for, influenced at first by Björnstjerne Björnson, the Norweigan novelist, he turned away from the English tradition in practice. All his life long he was to praise the Russians, French, Spanish, Norwegians, and Italians. Moreover, he disliked "the foolish joys of mere fable"—he agreed with Sartre in turning away from "the silly business of mere storytelling"; for the story-element in *Their Wedding Journey* was the least of Howells's cares. He was interested in the unfolding of character in action. His aim was to convey the texture of life in the intermingled play of natural people.

In this novel, written in the years following the Civil War, one sees the "more smiling aspects of life," although Howells speaks of the "shabby despots who govern New York and the swindling railroad kings" whom Henry Adams was exposing. Later, as the evils of American Life showed themselves more and more, Howells was constrained to write about them, and his novels grew more somber as Tolstoy and Ibsen worked upon him and he saw poverty and tragedy everywhere. But *Their Wedding Journey* remained to remind the reader of the American innocence of an earlier day when one could think "with tenderness of all the lives that have opened so fairly and the hopes that have reigned in glad young hearts." Henry Adams, writing of the book when it was first published, said, "Our descendants will find nowhere so faithful and pleasing a picture of our American existence. . . . Why should it not live? . . . If extreme and almost photographic truth to nature, and remarkable delicacy and lightness of touch, can give permanent life to a story, why should this one not be read with curiosity and enjoyment a hundred or two hundred years hence?" Theodore Dreiser agreed with Adams half a century later, and, as the novel approaches its hundredth year, many can still be found who agree with both.

Introduction to A *Hazard of New Fortunes*

Howells was fifty-three years old when he published A
Hazard of New Fortunes. Born in Ohio, he had lived in
Boston for a good part of twenty-five years, and, finally
feeling that it was "not life" but "death-in-life" there—for the
great literary days had long since passed—he had moved in
1889 to New York. This was the "hazard of new fortunes"
for Basil and Isabel March, the editor and his wife who appear in the novel and who have been living in Boston like
Howells and his wife, the originals of these fictitious persons.
Howells himself had been only, he said, a "naturalized
Bostonian," and his interests had shifted to "the one city
that belongs to the whole country," in the phrase of Fulkerson who also appears in the novel. Boston was no longer
the metropolis of writers, and the "vast, gay, shapeless"
New York scene, all novelty to Howells, gave him a quick-
ened interest in the life about him. The city seemed to him
inexhaustibly dramatic, all copy for Howells as for Stephen
Crane and many another younger man who hoped to write
the great American novel. With Howells the center of American letters shifted from Boston to New York.

Howells had been a poet before he became a novelist
and he had been, above all, a writer of travels. With his
Venetian Life he had had a great success, and he had
followed this with *Italian Journeys* before he wrote *Their
Wedding Journey* in 1872. Goldoni, the Venetian playwright,

Introduction to William Dean Howells' A *Hazard of New Fortunes*
by Van Wyck Brooks. Copyright © 1960 by Bantam Books, Inc.

had been his first master whose influence originally turned him from poetry to prose, showing him how to study people, all sorts of types and characters, making love, eating, singing, as one saw them in the streets. This adroit workman in human nature, natural, simple and merry, affected Howells especially as a writer of plays, so that his own comedies and farces abounded in situations that were drawn directly from Goldoni. Meanwhile, as consul for four years in Venice, with virtually nothing to do but write and study, Howells developed a shrewd eye for the traits of human nature, among the Venetians as among the American tourists. Keeping house with his wife and living in the Venetian way, he was brought into close contact with the life of the people, fishermen who stopped at the door, peddlers of firewood, chair-menders and glaziers, and the old woman who brought their milk in the morning. All this familiar knowledge appeared in his book *Venetian Life*; and at the same time as consul he studied the traveling Americans, many of them mothers and daughters in these Civil War years. The daughters, frequently charming, involved in complications both their mothers and the consul, as one saw in Howells's novel *A Foregone Conclusion*, and many of the types that Howells observed in the Venetian scene were to appear in his work for decades in the future. He was impressed by what he called the mystery of women's nerves, given as they often were to strategic headaches. He was to shatter the chivalric fiction of women's helpless nobility, for his women were to be frequently all subterfuge and artifice, mentally frank but sentimentally secret. There were those who felt that he libeled American womanhood, as they felt Henry James did in *Daisy Miller*; but for him, as for others in his time, the young girl was the most triumphant fact—as one saw in countless novels—in our civilization.

Howells's Venetian life prolonged itself in Cambridge, where he had settled in 1866, and where he soon joined the staff of *The Atlantic Monthly*, of which he was editor-in-chief for the next ten years. At first he saw Italy in Cambridge: Italian harpers came to the door, venders of plaster statuettes, a scissor-grinder from Lombardy, a little old

Genoese woman with packets of needles to sell, thread, pins, and tape. His first fictional work, *Suburban Sketches*, was full of Italian scenes at home, while it exhibited his gay, lighthearted early talent and the style, so nimble and fresh, that spread his reputation. His first novel, *Their Wedding Journey*, appeared shortly after. Journeys, whether abroad or at home, were a specialty of Howells, and scenes of travel on boats and trains and in sleeping cars and parlor cars were a feature of his novels and stories in years to come. So were waiting rooms and summer hotels that brought together people from every corner of the country, East, South, and West, people who could seldom have met in less public places; for Howells, with his continental mind, was bent on assembling characters of all the sections and of all classes and types. Boats, trains, and hotels were the inevitable settings for an all-American novelist at that moment.

Now Howells was attempting something new when he wrote *Their Wedding Journey*. He was attempting to present, for the first time, with Henry James, actual American characters in their habit as they were, unlike the "females" of Fenimore Cooper, the types of Mrs. Stowe or even the romanticized characters of Hawthorne. Henry Adams, reviewing the book, noted the author's success in realizing aspects of the native life. "Our descendants," Adams said, "will find nowhere so faithful and pleasing a picture of our American existence"; and he added, "Why should it not live? If extreme and almost photographic truth to nature and remarkable delicacy and lightness of touch can give permanent life to a story, why should this one not be read with curiosity and enjoyment a hundred or two hundred years hence?" Howells greatly admired Björnstjerne Björnson, who was creating at this time, with one or two others, a modern literature for Norway, and he delighted in Björnson's art of representing people with a few distinct and simple touches. Fullness in brevity might have been Björnson's motto, and Howells himself had been anxious to escape from the "heavy and awkward traditions of the craft" that George Eliot and Dickens perpetuated. He was, in short, in reaction against the "bad school we were all brought up in," the school of the English novelists whom everyone read, and he turned away from them to the continental novelists, Russian, French, Norwegian, Italian, and Spanish. Their fiction was the only living movement in imaginative literature, Howells was soon to write in one of his essays. The realism of his own early novels exemplified this movement, as they excelled also in brevity and lightness.

Meanwhile, Howells turned upon Boston the all-observant eye that he had developed during the years in Venice, exploring the New England capital at about the moment when his friend Henry James was exploring London. There was the Boston of the Italians, reflected in *Suburban Sketches*, the Boston of isms in *The Undiscovered Country*, the Boston of the newspaper world caught in *A Modern Instance*, and the Boston of boardinghouses in *The Minister's Charge*. The Boston mind still had, he said, an "idealizing tendency," unlike the "realizing tendency" of New York, and Howells therefore saw the city with a keener eye than any native Bostonian could have seen it. He saw the old Bostonians, the Bellinghams and Coreys, and the newly-rich countrypeople who had moved into town and sometimes became involved with the world of fashion, as one saw in *The Rise of Silas Lapham*. Howells's Boston novels, the fine and the not so good, abounded in first-rate portraits of many types, the minister, Lemuel, the country boy, Bromfield Corey, the Boston swell, and especially Lapham, his wife and his two daughters. All these characters, and many others, were particularized and strikingly real, so that Howells was always to be recalled as the social historian of Boston of the seventies, eighties, and nineties of the nineteenth century. With a thousand subtle touches, he pictured in his *comédie humaine* a world that had not been known to outsiders before.

About this time Howells spoke of "the more smiling aspects of life" as being, he said, "the more American," a phrase that was seriously held against him especially in a post-world-war time when the "power of blackness" governed the imagination. But after the Civil War, except in the unhappy South, confidence and hope were the notes of

American life everywhere; and, moreover, Howells had soon become aware of the evils that abounded in the life of the country. Many of his later novels dwelt on these evils—for one, *The Son of Royal Langbrith*, a fine psychological story that might well have made an Ibsen play. The dead manufacturer Langbrith had been a scoundrel, although he was the benefactor of the New England milltown, and the novel showed the tragic results of "letting lying dogs sleep," concealing the truth from the son who worshipped him. *The Quality of Mercy* was another tragic tale, the story of a defaulter, a type of the moment; and in certain books like *A Traveller from Altruria* Howells seemed even to reject the claims of American society altogether. America was "Egoria" in this book, the opposite of "Altruria"—there people lived *upon* instead of for one another—and one witnessed there the squalid struggle of a plutocratic world where "the man who needs a dinner is the man who is never asked to dine." In short, in this romance, American life is a nightmare that really seems to have no smiling aspects, though the charge of an easy optimism continued to be laid against Howells by critics who had often never read him. America is "so ugly it *hurts*," he wrote to a friend on his return from Europe, at a time when he was too well aware of the slovenly speech of his countrymen, their "flat wooden tones" and the "bottomless pit" of their manners. It was true that, beside the "veteran duplicities of histrionic Europe," Howells liked the directness and sincerity he found at home, and he never lost his belief in "the true state" that America was "destined yet to see established."

Many years before this, in 1874, in fact—Howells had had a brief correspondence with Turgenev. The Russian novelist had read his *Venetian Life* and *A Chance Acquaintance*, and he wrote, "Your literary physiognomy is a most sympathetic one . . . natural, simple and clear . . . full of unobtrusive poetry and fine humour." Turgenev had been drawn to American writers, he had read Bret Harte, Hawthorne, and Whitman, and sixteen translations of his own work had appeared in the United States when only five or six had been published in England. Turgenev's

Natalie, Elena, and Lisa had seemed to many like American cult, and for Howells, as largely for Henry James, he was "the man who has set the standard for the novel of the future." Howells continued, "Life showed itself to me in different colours after I had once read Turgenev; it became more serious, more awful and with mystical responsibilities I had not known before my gay American horizons were bathed in the vast melancholy of the Slav, patient, agnostic, truthful." Turgenev's elevation and the poetry of all he wrote had a profound effect on the mind of Howells, both deepening his point of view and confirming his own taste for a small group of characters in the composition of a novel. Owing very largely to the vacancy of our social life, we excel, said Howells, in small pieces with three or four figures; and his own earlier novels had resembled Turgenev's in this respect. It was partly Turgenev who led Howells's mind away from the smiling aspects to the graver aspects of American life. He had shown in A Modern Instance some of the "sad things" that generally formed the substance of Turgenev's novels.

For Howells the novelist's business was "to see and record," and during all his later life he had a special feeling for the Russians from Gogol to Gorky and Artzybasheff. The same ideal was continuous, he said, "in that wonderful Slavic race," and, faithful as he was to the Spanish and Italian realists, Giovanni Verga, Galdós, and Valdés, he owed most to Tolstoy, reading whom was for him a sort of religious experience, really a conversion. While he delighted in Hardy and Zola—"the greatest poet of his day"—in Anthony Trollope, Henry James, and Stendhal, Tolstoy's "heart-searching books," he wrote, were worth all other novels and gave both doing and being a new meaning and motive. Tolstoy prepared him for socialism, which he adopted in 1887, about the time when he moved from Boston to New York and when he was interested too in Bellamy's Looking Backward, Henry George's Progress and Poverty and the Fabian Essays. From that time forward, Howells was hostile to the ideals of a business world, abounding in millionaires and, still more, in tramps, and he felt that American society was coming out all wrong unless it based itself anew on a real equality. He wrote two or three Tolstoyan novels—*Annie Kilburn* and *The Minister's Charge*—and socialist or Tolstoyan characters appeared in several of his later books, Lindau in *A Hazard of New Fortunes* and David Hughes in *The World of Chance*. But the explicitly Tolstoyan novels were not very good, for Howells lost his novelist's detachment in his treatment of these themes that appealed so closely to his heart. He was at his best in other novels in which the search for justice appeared as only one of the touchstones of existence.

Of these *A Hazard of New Fortunes* was the finest, undoubtedly, the longest of Howells's novels and by far the most complex in theme, in the range of characters, in motives, and settings. "You are less *big* than Zola," Henry James wrote to him, apropos of this novel, which appeared in 1890, "but you are ever so much less clumsy and more really various," and the variety in this novel was Howells's reflection of the complex metropolitan note and scene. The ingenious device of a magazine brought all the characters together, for "Every Other Week" served as a focus, with Basil March as the editor, Dryfoos as the angel, and Fulkerson as the impresario. About this magazine Howells assembled types of a dozen worlds, the new and the old South, the West, the Leightons from New England, Lindau, the German socialist translator. Then there is Kendricks, the admirer of Baudelaire and Flaubert who is always hoping himself to write a novel, Margaret Vance of the fashionable world, the Dryfoos girls and their brother Conrad, and Angus Beaton, the irresponsible painter. Howells departed here from his earlier fictional method of assembling, in Turgenev's manner, a small group of people, and these main characters were surrounded by the "foreigners" who gave New York the touch-and-go picturesqueness that appealed to Howells. For New York, however cosmopolitan, was in the eighteen-nineties still a basically "old American" or Anglo-Saxon city. One saw behind the story the German, French, and Spanish faces that Howells had noted everywhere, not to mention the scenes of the later "Ashcan" painters, John Sloan and Everett Shinn, whom he knew and admired: there were the Swiss châlets of the elevated railway, the vistas of shabby side streets, the old hip-roofed houses that were still remaining. Basil March himself preferred the East side to the West side lines because they "raced into the gay ugliness, the shapeless, graceful, reckless picturesqueness of the Bowery," and he delighted in the "primo tenore" statue of Garibaldi in Washington Square and the cockneyish quality of the ballad-sellers. There was much of the painter in Howells, and this trait appeared in *A Hazard of New Fortunes* more than in any other of his novels.

"The most vital of my fictions," Howells called this book, and no other novel ever contained so much of the life of New York when the nineteenth century was closing. Comic and tragic by turns, it abounded in dramatic scenes, like the death of Conrad in the streetcar strike and the great dinner at which Dryfoos and Lindau violently confront one another's fixed ideas. It is a great sweep of life that Howells brings before us, natural, concrete, varied, and intensely real, and the characters, minutely particularized, both timeless and of their time, unite a moment of the past with our actual present. Following the story, we live it intensely as if it were taking place under our own eyes, and one could imagine no greater tribute to Howells's veracious imagination.

Introduction to *The Damnation of Theron Ware*

The Damnation of Theron Ware is a first-rate novel by an otherwise little-known author, a "country boy of genius," as Louise Imogen Guiney called him, who had grown up in the Mohawk valley. Harold Frederic edited newspapers in Utica and Albany before he went to London as the correspondent of the *New York Times,* and he lived in England for fourteen years, from 1884 to 1898, when he died at the age of forty-two. He wrote nine novels, including three romances of England, largely stories about "lost heirs"—the theme of *The American Claimant* and other stories of the time. But the tale of Theron Ware was Frederic's only fine book—one that followed the prescription of his master, William Dean Howells. The leader of the American realists said, "Write about the life you know best"; and the Octavius of the novel was a Mohawk valley town that might have been Utica, Frederic's birthplace.

Theron Ware is a young Methodist minister who is both ambitious and attractive. He is a new type, no longer a fighting pioneer like the primitive Wesleyans who appear at the Nedahma Conference, old worn-out preachers with trembling hands who had given their lives to poverty and the wearing toil of itinerant missions through rude frontier settlements. But, aspiring to become a "pulpit orator," he gradually goes to pieces when he is brought into contact

Introduction by Van Wyck Brooks to *The Damnation of Theron Ware* by Harold Frederic. Copyright © 1962, Fawcett Publications, Inc., and reprinted by permission of Fawcett Publications.

with science, art, and Celia Madden. His congregation, as the trustees say, wants "straight-out, flatfooted hell," and "no book-learnin' or dictionary words in our pulpit." The trustees even object to the roses in the bonnet of poor young Mrs. Ware, the faithful wife who stands by her malleable husband. Theron sets out, with a few Methodist manuals, to write a great book, a study of the patriarch Abraham, but, meeting Dr. Ledsmar, the learned anthropologist, he is obliged to feel that he is an untutored country lout. He is more and more bewildered as he falls in with a complex world that also exists in the town of Octavius—especially Father Forbes, the cultivated Irish Catholic priest, and the red-haired Celia, daughter of the richest man in the town. A friend of Dr. Ledsmar, the equally learned Father Forbes speaks of the "Christ-myth" and the symbolic truth of religion; and Celia, organist at the Catholic church, the exotic girl who personifies art, bestows a kiss upon Theron and completes his downfall. He had come to see himself as a "brother of Renan and Chopin," no longer a Methodist at all. Theron had thought of the Irish as ignorant, squalid and brutal—the usual feeling about them in provincial Americans of the time—and Celia and Father Forbes are the first well-educated people he has met, the first to give him a notion of intellectual culture. His fundamentalism crumbles away, and, infatuated with the cynical Celia and the scholarly cosmopolitan priest, he slides downhill "submerged in a bath of disgrace."

The characters in the novel are solidly real, not least the Madden family in their magnificent dwelling—the rich old father, an Irish peasant, and his disreputable son, on whose behalf Celia and Father Forbes go to New York together. When Theron Ware follows them on the same train, suspicious of their relations, he is inviting the final collapse from which he is rescued by the fund-raisers, Sister and Brother Soulsby. This old theater-girl of the touring circuits and the "regular bad old rooster," the good-hearted fraud of a husband who works with her, knowing that Theron should never have been a minister, get him a job as a real-estate agent in Seattle. They have saved his church in Octavius and they save him. The cheerful and motherly Sister Soulsby, who did not go in for cant and who had had "a little turn with a grand jury," was a type of the moment who believed in being a "good" fraud and who urged Theron to be a good fraud also. Father Forbes and Dr. Ledsmar are fully rounded characters who throw into relief the flabbiness of Theron—the priest by his integrity and worldly wisdom, the doctor by the depth of his erudition. Henry Adams might have said that in Frederic's Celia Madden, as well as in the stories of Bret Harte, an American author had insisted on the power of sex, used not for "sentiment" but for "force"; more even than the two learned men who dishevel his theology, she bemuses the addle-headed Theron.

When the novelist Conrad called Harold Frederic "a notable journalist who had written some novels," he had probably not read *The Damnation of Theron Ware*. As a journalist, Frederic's chief exploit had been to go to Russia to study the mistreatment of the Jews there, and he described in *The New Exodus* the rebarbarization of Russia that had hunted the Jews in pogroms like so many hares. But when Stephen Crane arrived in England in 1897, Frederic was one of the two men he wanted most to meet—the author who had published the year before *The Damnation of Theron Ware*, the novel that was called in England *Illumination*. It was Harold Frederic who urged Crane to write *Active Service*, a romantic story of the Greco-Turkish war, a weak little novel with fine images of warfare. Frederic's life was ending on a note of scandal. The mistress for whom he had left his wife and who was a Christian Scientist had caused him to abjure medicine and doctors. She was tried but acquitted for manslaughter after his death. This was only two years after he had published his best novel, one of the finest novels of its American decade.

Introduction to *Main-Travelled Roads*

Hamlin Garland was a follower of Howells, who said that a novelist should deal with the life he knows best and cares the most about. In fact, according to Eugene Field, who preferred to write about valorous knights, fairy godmothers, and especially children, Howells was the "only bad habit" of Garland. At that time both Field and Garland were living in Chicago, but Garland himself had spent several years in Boston before he began to write at all. He had taken the "back trail," to the amazement of the westward-streaming millions for whom the sunset sky stood for promise and romance, and, alone and poor in the "cradle of liberty," he had studied Darwin and John Fiske, absorbing the ideas of Taine about environment, race, and moment. Then he had fallen in with Howells, who turned his mind back to the prairies on which he had grown up, and, still in Boston, he began to put together the stories he collected in *Main-Travelled Roads*.

Garland had come from the Middle Border, one of the last of the Westerners for whom Boston was the literary metropolis. His family had moved from Wisconsin to Iowa, then to Minnesota and then to South Dakota, but Garland himself refused to follow, although for a winter he took up a claim of his own. He had been for a while in charge of his father's farm, and Garland remembered the

Introduction by Van Wyck Brooks to *Main-Travelled Roads* by Hamlin Garland. Copyright © 1961, Fawcett Publications, Inc., and reprinted by permission of Fawcett Publications.

feeling of adventure when his family moved to the remoter West and the unploughed places of the unsettled prairie. The Garland cabin was a house of song, for his maternal uncles were all musicians, but one and all were subject to moods of heartache and loneliness, and the father resented the stumps that impeded his plough. Garland resolved to leave his shack on the windswept plain, go to Massachusetts —which no other plainsman before him had done by choice —and fit himself to teach.

He had thought the plains life dull and petty; only when he came back, after talking with Howells, did he see the mark of tragedy elsewhere. He had visited Walt Whitman in Camden and become a disciple of Henry George, whose *Progress and Poverty* he had studied in his prairie shack. Now, returning from the East, he found his mother imprisoned in a dismal cabin on a treeless plain. He saw the all-pervading poverty and weariness in these households of toil; he understood the Populist revolt of the farmers.

Garland's collection of stories of farm-life on the prairie was new at the time in its grim candor. *Main-Travelled Roads* was published in 1891, and only E. W. Howe's *Story of a Country Town* anticipated this as a tale of arid village life. Garland was preparing the way for the darker school of realism that followed the "folksy" softness of James Whitcomb Riley. He described his own method as "veritism," or work that could be verified in comparison with facts.

In later stories, Garland followed the younger people to the mountain West, the Rockies, Wyoming, Colorado, where life among the Indians and the ranchmen of the "high country" was more exhilarating, adventurous and bold. He became a more popular storyteller, but he had lost his own best theme: the tragic feeling that had given depth to his first rude tales of the old home scenes. Later still, in a series of books of autobiography, he returned to the Iowa plains and the prairies of Dakota. In *A Son of the Middle Border* and the volumes that succeeded it, he related the life of his family, who, had gone west from Maine, settling in the Western coulees among Indians and wolves. There he described again the contests of skill and strength, the dancing in the barn on Saturday nights, the country fiddlers who shared in the hog-killings, pitched grain, and liked to work at the threshing machine. Garland remembered Daddy Deering in his rusty pantaloons, playing Irish love songs and Scottish airs, welcome in the early days when he pleased the boys and girls for whom his music was not too monotonous and simple. But he had observed the weedy fields, the farmhouses, lonely and boxlike, the tired, bedraggled women who were filling the asylums, with nothing to read and no music in their poor little cabins on a desolate prairie where life was devoid of anything but work and the air fell into silence with the coming of night.

Most of the stories in *Main-Travelled Roads* were in harmony with a scene in which people were caught like flies in a pan of molasses, with a home of toil at one end of the road and a dull little town at the other. In one tale the prosperous actor-son who had left the homestead ten years earlier, returned too late to rescue the family he had neglected. The old farm had been sold. His mother was living on in dumb despair; his younger brother was sullenly struggling to wrest a meager livelihood from the soil. In an agony of remorse, the elder son buys back the old homestead so that his mother, at least, can have some comfort. In another story a lover comes back to find the girl with whom he had quarreled, a broken farm drudge, worn out at thirty; in still another an old farmwife who had never had a day to herself takes a month off to revisit the home of her childhood. For twenty-three years she has stuck to the stove and the churn and has had to come home from every picnic to milk the cows and get supper for the menfolk.

But there is great variety in these stories, just the same; and, amid all the sorrow and resignation, and the cold days in the colorless farmhouses, there is a constant play of affection and humor.

Introduction to *McTeague*

Frank Norris died when he was thirty-two, but into those three decades he succeeded in packing an all but unparalleled measure of living and writing. Born in Chicago in 1870, the son of a prosperous business man, he was taken at fifteen to San Francisco. Then, going to Paris at seventeen as an art student, he returned to study at Berkeley and at Harvard. He reported the Boer war in South Africa, strongly supporting the British side, and the Spanish-American War in Cuba, where he fell in with Stephen Crane, whose life and work were similar—and dissimilar—to his own. Norris and Crane were almost exactly contemporaries. Both had studied low life in New York or San Francisco, as naturalists with different tendencies and aims, and Norris criticized the absence in Crane of the Zolaesque details that meant so much to him in his own writing. By no means a craftsman in words, as Crane was, Norris was under the spell of Zola, and, lacking altogether Crane's verbal distinction, he had his own wider sweep and force. He was a master of documentation, and in this he resembled Theodore Dreiser, whose *Sister Carrie* he acclaimed when he worked for a while as a publisher's reader in New York.

For Norris, San Francisco was one of the American "story cities," a "place where things can happen," as Kipling had felt; and Norris' mind returned to it when he gave up

Introduction by Van Wyck Brooks to *McTeague* by Frank Norris. Copyright © 1960, Fawcett Publications, Inc., and reprinted by permission of Fawcett Publications.

his early dream of painting and writing mediaeval romances in Paris. He strolled about the paths of the campus at Berkeley with the yellow-backed novels of Zola under his arm, and, meanwhile, he studied the waterfront—where Jack London had grown up—and the riverboats and the schooners from Australia and Asia. He haunted the narrow streets and the rickety dwellings of Chinatown, with their shaky stairways, warrens, passages, and alleys, and he talked with sailors and prostitutes in saloons and brothels of the Barbary Coast, and visited the mines in the Sierras where McTeague had worked. In preparation for his "trilogy of the wheat," and especially *The Octopus*, he fraternized with cow punchers, stage drivers, and prospectors, and he spent two months on a ranch where he could watch the growth and the harvesting of the grain. Later, before he wrote *The Pit*, he returned to Chicago for a while to make a study there of the wheat exchange. Then he made a close study, in San Francisco, of the mean streets one sees in *McTeague*, where small tradespeople live over their shops —cheap restaurants, barber shops, stationers, and corner "drugstores. It was on Polk Street that McTeague had his "dental parlors," with a great gold tooth outside the window and an odor of stale bedding and ether heavy in the air. There the oxlike dentist plied his trade with mallet-like red hands that were covered with a mat of yellow hair; and there he drowsed on Sundays in a fog of tobacco smoke while he played mournful tunes on the concertina.

Frank Norris accepted the naturalistic formula of his master Zola, according to which nothing exists but external forces, and McTeague sinks without a struggle when the authorities find that he has no licence and cannot practice. Grasping for money, the ruling passion in this book, he ends by murdering his wife who refused to part with the bag that contains her savings; and this is far from natural in a character whom the author has described as obliging, good-natured, and forgiving. To use the will is as natural as it is to forgo it; but the point is easily overlooked in the otherwise massive reality of this great picture of life that is called *McTeague*. Norris began to write the book when he was a student at Harvard, and this panorama of low life wears as well as ever, after sixty years and two generations. Maria, the Mexican servant girl, and rag-and-bone man Zerkow, and the German-Swiss family of Trina and her cousin Marcus are as vividly present in the reader's mind as the vaudeville show, the wedding, the picnic in the amusement park, and the bridal rooms. One cannot forget their banalities, their odors, their flavors, nor McTeague himself, the personification of Zola's *bête humaine*, his big legs heavy with ropes of muscle.

Frank Norris scorned the pale and bloodless in the romance of his time—"the literature of chambermaids," he called them—and with Jack London, and even before him, he was the founder of the "red-blood" school, the school of the "primordial," the "primeval." Norris had first found in Kipling that "splendid brutal bullying spirit" which he developed in two or three other novels, but before his early death he surrendered this arrogant worship of force, and acquired a humanitarian compassion and vision. His personal evolution, in short, was much like Ernest Hemingway's when he discovered that "no man is an island." The ranchman Annixter in *The Octopus* said, "I begin to see that a fellow can't live *for* himself any more than he can live *by* himself. He's got to think of others." This was the message of the poet Presley in that book, and it was the final message that Frank Norris left.

Introduction to *Maggie: A Girl of the Streets; George's Mother*

It was on the Bowery, Stephen Crane said once, that he got his "artistic education," and he said again that the Bowery was the only interesting place in New York and that nobody had written anything "sincere" about it. He himself slept in Bowery shelters and sat in tramp's clothes in Union Square, listening to the talk of real hoboes, and he stood all night in a March blizzard watching men waiting in a breadline. To experience sensations and convey them honestly was Stephen Crane's supreme ambition. But the author of *Maggie: A Girl of the Streets* was not the only American writer who, in the eighteen-nineties, was drawn to the slums. There were dozens who haunted the Bowery—Hutchins Hapgood was another of these—wishing to know "how the other half lives" or seeking Gorky's "creatures that once were man": they had both an interest in the types there and the *nostalgie de la boue* that filled the minds of the Bohemians of Paris and London. For the American imagination, the rise of the great cities had replaced the village and the farm.

To Stephen Crane, "sincerity," or honesty, the word he sometimes used, was the rare desideratum in American writing, and his own possession of this trait made him what the novelist Wells called "the best writer of our generation." Reviewers of *Maggie*, as of *George's Mother*, the short novel

Introduction by Van Wyck Brooks to *Maggie: A Girl of the Streets; George's Mother* by Stephen Crane. Copyright © 1960, Fawcett Publications, Inc., and reprinted by permission of Fawcett Publications.

that followed it, accused the author of cynicism and cold-
ness because, in telling the story, he left the reader to invest
with sentiment the facts that he related barely and boldly.
Maggie herself, a pretty girl, the child of a drunken father
and mother seduced by a young bartender who soon tires of
her, wanders vaguely through the streets when her mother
turns her out, trying to make a living soliciting men. When
at last she drowns herself, her mother cries, "I'll forgive
her!" thus putting an end to the ironical story in which
Howells found "the fatal necessity which dominates Greek
tragedy." Howells, who virtually discovered Crane, also
said, "Here is a writer who has sprung into life fully armed."
He was armed largely, like Hemingway later, by the things
he did not say, and that, by his omissions, gave the story its
power. The book consisted in large part of verbal impressions of tenement scenes, the chaos of back yards, the side
doors of saloons from which children emerged with pails of
beer, of the sweatshops and soup kitchens in which Maggie
bloomed and George developed his swaggering histrionic
fancies.

Born in New Jersey, the son of a Methodist minister,
Stephen Crane lived to be only twenty-nine years old; but,
besides the Bowery, he saw life in Mexico, in the West, in
Cuba, in Greece, and latterly in England. There he became
a friend of Joseph Conrad and H. G. Wells. While many of
his stories dealt with boys, somewhat in the manner of
Mark Twain, he was best known for his writings about war,
the war that gave him a sense of life at its highest pitch and
challenged his skill in conveying sensations precisely. With
curiosity as his ruling passion, he took all manner of risks
in order to know "how it felt," and, both in Cuba and
Greece, he seemed to be courting death when he strolled
under fire between the lines. But when he wrote his first
war book, *The Red Badge of Courage,* he had actually never
experienced war at all. It was this book that made him the
fair-haired boy of the eighteen-nineties, the admired of
printers, old soldiers, editors, and reviewers, who felt, as
they read it, that bullets were whistling about and that they
themselves were shuffling in the mud in Henry Fleming's

shoes. Never, in any American story, had war seemed so actually present. The men ran "with starting eyes and sweating faces," falling "like bundles" when they were shot, and one saw, in one's excitement, "each blade of the green grass, bold and clear" and the roughness of the surface of the brown-gray trunks of the trees. One heard the woods crackle like straw on fire and the "cat-spit" sound of the bullets that kept pecking at the men. Yet Stephen Crane had merely pored over Winslow Homer's Civil War drawings in copies of the old *Harper's Weekly*. With the aid of a book or two, especially Tolstoy's *Sebastopol*, of which someone had given him a copy, it had all come out of his imagination. Stephen Crane was aware that war was not a pageant but mainly an affair of trying to sit still and keep warm, and this feeling of the homeliness and casualness of the battlefield gave the novel its quality of real life.

The seemingly impassive Stephen Crane was an inscrutable character whose general view of life was bitter and dark, as one could see in the poems he wrote when Howells had read Emily Dickinson aloud to him. *Black Riders*, negative and bleak, was a bridge between the romantic poets and the free-verse poets who were to follow; and Crane, the prose-writer, was also a bridge between the earlier realists and the more drastic writers of the next generation. Much modern American fiction descends alike from *Huckleberry Finn* and the tragic author of *Maggie, a Girl of the Streets*, who wrote about life and war before the world-war epoch began and pointed out the way to his successors.

Introduction to *Together*

There is no doubt that the best novel of Robert Herrick, *Together*, first published in 1908, contains most of the elements of a typical Herrick novel.

The work of a New Englander who spent most of his life as a professor at the University of Chicago, it abounds in the criticism of the big businessman who was characteristic of the age of Theodore Roosevelt. Most of the men in the novel are engaged in some form of business, but it is Steve Johnston, the failure, who is revealed as a really good man—like the veteran Colonel Price, one of the old-fashioned merchants whom Herrick admired and praised in several novels. He saw these pioneers of trade along the Western rivers as being generous and kind, fatherly toward their employees, unlike the new "damned money-getters" who got so little themselves out of their lives. John Lane, the principal character, the vice-president of a great railroad, is convicted by the government of corruption, but while technically dishonest in his work, he is otherwise a fine man, and his wife Isabelle ignores and misunderstands him. Though she is the daughter of Colonel Price, Isabelle knows nothing whatever of business. She knows only the difference between stocks and bonds—until the French-Canadian Dr. Renault brings her and Lane together.

Isabelle, the heiress whose unhappy marriage opens the

Introduction by Van Wyck Brooks to *Together* by Robert Herrick. Copyright © 1962, Fawcett Publications, Inc., and reprinted by permission of Fawcett Publications.

book, is only one of the women who appear in the story; but for most of these women existence has become a shifting panorama of surfaces as they try to add a meaning to their sterile lives. They are carried away by the doctrines of marriage which they find in Ibsen and Bernard Shaw, the cult of the ego and feminine development. "If it were not for America, for the Mississippi Valley," Herrick said, "Ibsen would have had a quiet grave and Shaw might have remained the Celtic buffoon." The work of their husbands is a mystery to these wives. They are victims of such fashionable practitioners as Dr. Potts, a god for neurasthenic women who finds in their souls hypocrisy and fear.

Dr. Renault, who has been laid low with tuberculosis, settles in Grosvenor Flat, a village in northern Vermont, and there he has his "life laboratory," a place for making over human character as well as human tissue. There the diseased, the twisted, the maimed, the inhibited, the incomplete are analyzed and slowly reconstructed, cured of "pavementitis"—the pavement itch—and returned to life clearminded and sane. In this haven of peace, among hills and woods, snowy expanses and frozen brooks, all that means merely comfort is wanting. There is nothing to suggest the froth of immediate living; and Isabelle, freed from her cult of the ego, comes to agree with the doctor that "life is good —all of it—for everybody." Losing her appetite for city life and those "huge, squirming, prodigal hives"—the great cities—she finally rejoins her husband and with him undertakes a new life on another frontier in Texas.

Together, is a long book, and many other characters complicate the story of the Lanes—among them Isabelle's brother, Vickers, who runs away to Italy with his mistress. There are also Margaret Pole, the Falkners, the Woodyards and the Senator, the old friend of Colonel Price; all "plastic," as Dr. Renault says, and all involved—in St. Louis or New York—with one another. But all are involved, most deeply, with Isabelle and John Lane, the ill-matched couple who come together at the end.

The book appeared when Theodore Roosevelt was President and "malefactors of great wealth" were much in the news, and this story of businessmen and their wives, so symptomatic of the time, retains its interest half a century later. Herrick foreshadowed the "muckraking" writers, as he paralleled Thorstein Veblen, who was also a professor in Chicago at the same time as Herrick and who would have understood the novelist's real heroes, the men who had "a purpose, a big end" before them.

Herrick disliked as profoundly the exploiters of the industrial world as he liked Jervis Thornton, the engineer, with his one small trunk that held all his possessions. What the austere Herrick admired was simple living and "the common lot, which is to live humbly and labour," a feeling of integrity that appeared in the characters of whom he approved, and who "lifted life something nearer to importance and beauty." He celebrated these types in all his novels —in Coburn, the bacteriologist, who has a laboratory in the Chicago slums; in Dr. Sommers, who resigns as partner of the fashionable humbug Lindsay; in others who dislike dishonesty, flimsiness, deceit.

Herrick especially abhorred waste, the subject of one of his last novels, the waste of the national resources that business entailed, the "conspicuous waste" of Veblen, who observed the Chicago scene with an eye that was still more bitter and sardonic. For Veblen, too, Chicago was an object lesson. On the other hand Herrick admired the old steelmaker who founded a school, as he admired Colonel Price, and his fine portraits of professors and the new intellectuals ranged over all the national scene.

Herrick believed in good workmanship just as Veblen did, and an industry that was divorced from politicians. For "detachment, poverty, suffering" were the "three rules of discipline that led from the bondage of squalor into beauty." And again, in his novel, *The Master of the Inn*, he celebrated a doctor like the doctor in *Together* who helps men and women to detach themselves from the confusions of modern life.

Introduction to *Earth Memories*

It was in 1921 that I first saw Llewelyn Powys, in the New York office of the *Freeman*. He had just come from Africa, where, for five years, he had managed a sheep and cattle ranch on the shore of Lake Elmenteita. One of a group of brothers and sisters who were all but prodigiously gifted, with two great English poets among their forbears— John Donne and William Cowper—he was already at work on the sketches of African life that soon announced a master of English prose. With his bright curly hair and weathered features and his deep-set eyes that were used to the glare of the sun, with his rough gray woolen coat and sprig of holly, he had an old-country look that suggested some shaggy god in exile, an Apollo playing the shepherd in a faraway land.

When, later, he used to walk to Westport, by the Wolf Pit Road and Nash's Pond—for he was a notable wayfarer and he often stayed at Norwalk—he gave me this impression still more strongly. He was at home in the country, and only there. Well as he knew cities, and many of them, from London to Jerusalem and San Francisco, he had nothing whatever in common with their tone and temper. Men who had forgotten how to hunt or to grow corn or catch wild

Introduction by Van Wyck Brooks to *Earth Memories* by Llewelyn Powys. New York: W. W. Norton & Co., 1938. (Brooks wrote a very short preface to another of Powys's works, *Thirteen Worthies*, 1923, reprinted Freeport, N. Y.: Books for Libraries Press, Inc., 1966.) Permission to reprint granted by Mrs. Gladys Brooks and Malcolm Elwin, biographer and literary executor of L. Powys, through his representatives, Laurence Pollinger Ltd.

fowl were mechanical dolls to this lover of life. He preferred farm laborers or gypsies. One could scarcely imagine him reading a newspaper—his style is untouched by newspaperese; and his speech was full of rustic saws and rhymes. But even in his rusticity there was something strange, a vague hint of the prehistoric that clung to his personality, with the ripeness of his culture and the sweetness of his courtesy. If the day was cold, he sometimes wore the old plaid shawl that had once belonged to the poet Edward FitzGerald, the friend of his great-uncle, "old Donne." Cold or not, the day seemed always May Day. He had contrived to find a little knot of field flowers where no other eye had seen them by the road, and he had brought spring with him in his hand. But this spring, in his talk and presence, recalled the pagan rites of Druids and the ancient earth-worship of the flint-men. It was not the spring of modern poets, or even of Herrick or Shakespeare, although Powys repeats their note in many essays. It evoked the first maypoles in the dawn of England, the smell of goats, the chants of the diviners in days when men whose bones lie under barrows, mad in their zest for living, adored the sun.

At that time, no one knew Llewelyn Powys as the formidable pagan thinker he has since become. He had not yet published *The Cradle of God*, that wonderful meditation on the biblical story, so grave and often sublime, perhaps the most deeply reasoned of all his writings. While few true believers have embraced the story with any such poetic understanding, he follows Ecclesiastes there as elsewhere: "For the living know that they shall die, but the dead know not anything." In half a dozen other books, he reiterates this with a splendid eloquence. "Brief as a rainbow your dream also will be. There is no clemency, no reprieve, no escape; no, not for the strongest heart deep mortised in life." There is no existence save that of the senses, no acceptable state of consciousness aside from this, and the senses die with the beasts of the field—such is the burden of his thinking. One doubts if there has been a writer since Robert Burton and Thomas Browne in whom the contrast of life and death has inspired more magnificent periods. But why this passion of

negation? It suggests an immense vitality incomparably men-
aced, and that this is the case we can see in his beautiful
essays in autobiography, especially *Skin for Skin* and *Black
Laughter*. In more than one sense, FitzGerald's mantle has
fallen upon his shoulders, for Omar's "phantom Caravan"
never included a mighty hunter with a keener sense than his
of the "bird of time." But he himself has said, "I cannot
reconcile myself to the lack of gusto" that FitzGerald dis-
plays in his quatrains, their wan Pre-Raphaelite sadness; and
his own gusto, his thirst for life, is beyond all measure virile
and eager. When such a man for thirty years dwells in the
constant presence of death, he may well find the light sweet
and rejoice that his eyes behold the sun. When every hour of
every day has been snatched from the hand of fate, the
things of the hour and the day are beyond all price. It is
true that in some minds, in these conditions, the super-
sensual world becomes all-important; and perhaps for most
men, under any conditions, a philosophy of the senses in insufficient. But most of the pessimists—for Powys is a pessi-
mist—are so because they find life insufficient, whereas for
him existence is a daily rapture.

It might not be difficult, running through Powys's various
books, to trace the natural history of his view of life. In the
Swiss sanitarium, which he describes in *Skin for Skin*, he first
became convinced that "nothing mattered." To possess the
present, to see, to hear, to taste, to touch, this was enough
for a young man who believed that he was dying and who
could almost feel his nostrils, mouth and earholes bunged
with potter's clay. His African adventure accentuated this
animal faith. "Kill! kill! kill!" was the rhythm of existence
there, "hand against hide, claw against horn, beak against
fur." In the trees moulting vultures waited, and the jackal
and hyena prowled at night. Every game-path and open glen
was "frequented by silent-footed shadows on their eternal
quest for blood," and life was "a perpetual pursuit, a perpetual flight." There chance was the only law, and the past
was nothing, the future nothing. All nature seemed to cry,
"Seize the moment"; and Llewelyn Powys's writings have
shown us with what superb and reckless courage a man can

hold this faith and act upon it. No one has ever lived more dangerously, and few indeed are the modern writers who have drawn such a harvest of joy from their moment of life. As sensitive as a hare in the brush or a dace switching his tail in some English river, he has thrown the huntsman off the scent and eluded the fisherman's hook, while snuffing the sun-soaked earth and exulting in wind and water. His astonishing gift of metaphor and the richness of his language are proofs of this alertness of the senses; and with what zest he absorbs new places and new atmospheres, how expert he is in describing new sensations! There are passages in his travel-writings about Africa and the Rocky Mountains, Palestine, Switzerland and Capri that fairly take one's breath away. One feels as if these places had never been seen before, so startling are the reports of his "rabble senses." What reader can ever forget, for instance, the chapter in *Black Laughter* in which the "man of God" appears in his hut at night?—the witch doctor's cry outside, with "all the lunatic misery of the debased outraged soul of the African Negro," the motionless form that invades the room with its odor of rotting blood and flesh and the footprints stamped in the dust of the threshold, visible with the rising sun, one a foot with toes, the other a foot with claws. No palate was ever more sensitive to the wine of life, however the wine may be mingled at moments with gall.

Wherever Llewelyn Powys has lived, his mind has always turned towards England, the homeland that haunts him like a passion. Under the stars in the African jungle, poring over Robert Burton, whose rhythms have left long traces in his style—a style that is often archaic and always rare in texture —he dreamed of English gardens. In New York, in the clattering streets, he would see the cuckoo perched singing on the top of Sandsfoot Castle. He can always regain serenity, he says in one of his essays, by thinking of the playground of his childhood, the pear trees of Montacute Vicarage. High as his fever may be, the memory of this enchanted ground quiets his pulse in a moment; and his pictures of England suggest the eye of the convalescent, as if the world had been reborn for him. They are full of an all but miraculous freshness. He has told us with what delight, returning home, after his exile in Switzerland, when all his sensibilities had been sharpened by illness, he absorbed the sights and sounds of the Somerset meadows, how he came to know every lane and bypath, the character of each field-gate, the gap in every hedge, the alder-shaded pools, and grass-strewn bartons. Scrambling about the high chalk cliffs with the rain lashing against his face, he studied every rock and ledge of curlews, marveling over the gleaming pebbles, the cries of the gulls at dawn and the old stone circles of the Druids. In all the years that have passed since then he has kept his astonishing sensitivity, as the readers of this volume will discover. Indeed, he perceives more acutely than ever the homestead and the farmwain, the glittering dew on spider's web and burdock, the barking of foxes at twilight and every common earthy odor the smell of the fur of water rats and of horses' backs hot in the sun. He can tell you the sound of a hare drinking in some dreamy meadow where owls with clutching pounces float from tree to tree. England for Powys is still a mirage-world, quivering with yellow sunshine and hayfield grasses. It inspires in him that "heightened awareness of the poetry of existence" which he never ceases to praise as the true religion.

Beneath this sensuous England there are other Englands that have left their deposit in his mind. One feels in his pages depths upon depths of historic experience, a life of the heart and the soul as well as the instincts that carries one back to the men of the old stone circles. I have said that a hint of the prehistoric clings to his personality. Is it because he retains some trace of every epoch, or because his interior world knows nothing of time? A deeply compassionate nature, he is indifferent to secular interests. "We should grow less involved in society," he says in *Damnable Opinions*, "and more deeply involved in existence." His chosen companions are those for whom "existence" is incomparably more engrossing than the things of the world, the fisherman, peasants and shepherds for whom time has no reality and who live, as he wishes to live, in the fugitive moment. Deeply akin as he is to these earthbound natures, he shares their poetry and wisdom. But let no one suppose that Llewelyn Powys is merely another nature-writer, eloquent, observant, and persuasive. He has something to say to this age of despair and darkness, an age in which writers in all the tongues of Babel repeat that life is futile and worse than nothing. It may be that only a man who has had to fight for existence can prize it and exult in it as he does, beating his forehead upon the grass in jubilant acquiescence and uttering daily paeans to the earth and the sun. All the more should we cherish his will and his courage and the noble and beautiful art that permits us to share them.

Introduction to *Journey into the Self: Being the Letters, Papers & Journals of Leo Stein*

When, at the age of seventy-five, Leo Stein died in 1947, he had become a legendary figure, partly because of the distance that lends enchantment to Americans who spend their lives in Europe. I saw him only once or twice, in the days of the *Seven Arts*, to which he contributed two papers, days when —a painter and philosopher of sorts—he was rather a personage than anything else, although he suggested great reserves of wisdom. He obviously knew he was somebody, for "if you are doing the latest thing," Leo Stein wrote in later years, "you can feel at least a little bit important," and the limelight had been turned on him and Gertrude Stein, his sister, because of their unique connection with "modern art." They were close friends of the leaders of the movement in Paris and had even brought Picasso and Matisse together. Having the means to buy their pictures, the Steins had a room to show them in that soon became one of the sights of Paris, where Leo, discovering Cézanne for himself, had bought in 1902 the Cézanne that became the nucleus of their collection. There were as many, first or last, who claimed to have discovered modern art as there were cities that claimed to be the birthplace of Homer, but Leo Stein was no doubt the first, as he said, to recognize that Picasso and Matisse together were "the two important men." While Gertrude, sharing their point of view, tried to write in conjunction with

Introduction by Van Wyck Brooks from *Journey into the Self: Being the Letters, Papers & Journals of Leo Stein*, ed. by Edmund Fuller. © 1950 by the Estate of Leo D. Stein, Deceased. Used by permission of Crown Publishers, Inc.

them, endeavoring to parallel in words their effects in paint, Leo Stein, in the rue de Fleurus, expounded the movement to visitors who seldom knew anything outside the official salons. He felt, as he said once, "like a Columbus setting sail for a world beyond the world."

When I saw him in 1917, Gertrude Stein's fame was rapidly growing and Leo Stein merely shared the limelight with her, although he had more or less broken with her— "disaggregated" himself, as he put it—and gone to Florence where he was eventually to die. When Picasso entered his cubist phase, Leo Stein had lost interest in him, feeling that cubism was the "intellectual product of the unintellectual," who should "manifest themselves on a merely intelligent plane." Whether he was right or wrong in this, he was nothing himself if not intellectual, while his literary tastes were classical, even severely, so that he could not "take Gertrude seriously as a literary phenomenon"—he could not, as he said, "abide her stuff." As she was frankly out for glory, she could scarcely have missed his comradeship, surrounded as she was by others who swung incense before her, while he, pursuing his lonely way, was entirely good-natured in pointing out the mendacities in "Alice Toklas's fanciful romance." She had left him out of the picture, for reasons of her own which he understood, although he was the aesthetic discoverer far more than she was, but fortunately he was to live long enough to redress the balance in a book of his own and relate the true story of the "Paris episode." Meanwhile, he had little to show for himself in the years in which Gertrude rose to fame, twisting and turning as he was in a psychological bog, the victim of the "crippling neurosis" he described later that had started with something close to dementia praecox. He wrote a few essays and a crabbed book, the *ABC of Aesthetics*, and he toiled at painting off and on, convinced at times that he had found "the light in the darkness, the path in the desert, the way in the air where no way is." He felt in 1915 that he had discovered the "map" of his life and achieved the "goal of the quest psycho-analytic," but he suffered relapses one after another and could build nothing on his mind, which "came through only in fragments and distorted bits." Trying to live up to others' expectations of him, he felt that all the world was laughing at him—and laughing at his "psychology which never stopped"—and, feeling that he was a failure himself, he accomplished little enough to suggest the remarkable man he was all the time.

For the self-distrustful, introverted, analytic Leo Stein, with his air of an "old ram," as Mabel Dodge observed—she also said that Gertrude had a "laugh like a beefsteak"—was quite as remarkable in his way as the peremptory sister who had ruled the family roast since she was a girl. A twentieth-century Amiel who found himself late in life—when he wrote with serenity, lucidity, distinction, and grace—he had manifested through all these years the notable characteristics that flowered when he had passed three score and ten. A temperamental experimenter, born for an experimental age, he liked to test new methods of cooking and dancing, inventing fresh combinations of rhythms, pies that had never been heard of, and novel and unique variations of the flapjack and the pancake. He saw large possibilities in zucchini, for instance, and, devising a dish of zucchini with walnuts, he experimented with himself as well, a process through which in the end he found salvation. Planning at first to become a historian, in days when Gibbon was his ideal—when he was "satisfied to know and not concerned to understand"—he developed an encyclopedic mind and found himself scattered in too various a field, scientific, philosophic, and artistic. His mind was a riot of intellection as he went in for biology and found even trigonometry delightful, while he read mediaeval Latin, Italian poetry, German fiction, the *Gesta Romanorum*, Catullus, Boswell, Goethe. He suffered from a "plethora of things, ideas on all subjects," as he wrote in the days when he wrote well, although two strains of interest prevailed through all and over all, as he "thought like a scientist and saw like an artist." He was one of the pupils of William James who became a disciple of Freud, and his psychological interest was always acute, while he was passionately interested in art and had been since he was a boy, when he had begun to draw and "learned to see." He had found the meaning of composition in a canyon near their Oakland home where the Steins as children went for picnics and he had been struck by a group of live oaks that had, he saw, a special charm that was wholly due to its arrangement at a turn of the road. Becoming aware of composition, he looked for it on every hand and saw it in one poppy, for instance, that stood out in a meadow because of its peculiar position at the foot of a rock, and, comparing real apple trees with apple trees in etchings, he saw how the artist brought out the significance of their form. He had thus embarked in California on a long series of adventures of the mind that led him to seek living art with "value as form." He was to relate these in time in *Appreciation.*

For Leo Stein was a critic born, or, as one should say, a philosopher who thought about pictures almost too much to paint them, whose impressions, whether of art or nature, or the poetry he discussed so well, were instantly transmuted in his mind into ideas and reflections. Among his many pre-occupations, painting remained paramount—he said, "We are like the strings of a violin and a picture is the bow that sets us in motion"; and he who had spent radiant months in Paris, day after day, in his youth, at the Louvre, had early become a frequenter of art shops and dealers. At the first exhibitions of the modernists, he had looked at the Rouaults and Van Goghs as a botanist might look at the flora of an unknown land, and the character sketches of Matisse and Picasso that appeared in *Appreciation* had all the zest of the discoverer that, in fact, he was. This book, which Leo Stein described as a "little debauch in the realm of ideas," dwelt on the "cant of unreal appreciations"—the secondary kind of regard for the classics, for instance—and that variety of art-expression which is "merely the running of water down hill," since it follows the line of least resistance. Tension, for Leo Stein, was a prerequisite of living art, and so he disliked the music that "sang itself" and the words of bad poets that "slip into place as though they were greased" when they ought to "go into place as though they were jewelled." But he also disliked the current belief that art and society have nothing in common, that art has never served social ends. Was not Daumier socially significant? Was not Gavarni? And did not landscape in the nineteenth century, expressing the pantheism of the time, serve, like poetry, even the ends of worship? Appreciation, for Leo Stein, had a great role to play in the world. He saw society at the end of a road with only two alternatives, perpetual war or more appreciation, the appreciation of life and men that would lead people to give up the resistances and repressions that must otherwise lead them to fight.

When *Appreciation* at last appeared, Leo Stein had only a month to live, but he had arrived some years before at a state in which he no longer knew regrets, inhibitions, anxieties, discouragement, or fear. The "crusty deaf old man," he said, felt younger than he had ever felt and "younger than anyone whom one knows," his mental flexibility was greater than ever, his memory was better than it ever was—he was "growing," in short, "more plastic day by day." Repeating D. H. Lawrence's phrase, "Look, we have come through," he felt he had reached a perfect state of grace, though he found it really awful to awaken constantly more to life with so little time in which to reap his harvest. He had something, as he said, "four-square and as big as all out-doors" to say, everything but the years to work it out in, for he had become vocal as his insight matured—like William James and Berenson—and he took more and more delight in the choice of words. His painting flowed better than ever too, his "real occupation and primary interest," stirred latterly by the great Chinese landscape painters, while he took pains to express his thoughts with discriminating care and fit his words together like the works of a watch. He had begun a longer book, the story of his struggles and eventual triumph and the method of "continuous conversion" by which he had emerged from the long sickness that had largely unfitted him for life—the story of a mind that found itself, the fragments of which are printed here, with other memoranda and letters, in the *Journey into the Self*. This book reveals a personality that many will find more sympathetic, and even perhaps more valid, than his better-known sister's; and it seems to me beyond a doubt that Leo Stein, as one sees him here, was one of the most interesting men of the passing generation. His passion for ideas, his sensibility, the scrupulous honesty of his mind will constitute for many an abiding charm, and his life had the kind of happy ending that modern men can understand and even find reassurance in contemplating.

Preface to *The Silent Traveller in New York*

About a dozen years ago a book appeared in England that was called *The Silent Traveller in Lakeland*. It was the work of a Chinese painter and writer who had been for nearly five years a magistrate and district governor in his native city of Kiukiang on the Yangtse river. With an added interest of his own in scenery and animals, Mr. Chiang Yee followed in the footsteps of his father, an able amateur painter of flowers and birds, and he and his friends on walking trips had sketched and improvised poems as well at picturesque and legendary spots in the mountains. He had watched the sunrise from various peaks, especially Lu mountain near Kiukiang, renowned for its wild waterfalls and rocky scenes which the great Chinese poets and artists had sung and painted. The "Silent Traveller," the title that Mr. Chiang Yee adopted, was a translation of his Chinese pen name, which might have been literally rendered as "Dumb Walking Man." His work as a civil servant had kept him talking day and night, and, glad enough to escape from this, he had chosen a name that was not unlike the common phrase for a roaming Buddhist monk. Mr. Chiang Yee arrived in England in 1933, where he has lived ever since, appearing in a series of illustrated books as the "Silent Traveller" in London, Oxford, Edinburgh, and the Yorkshire dales. He had explored first, as Mr. Herbert Read said in his preface to

Preface by Van Wyck Brooks to *The Silent Traveller in New York* by Chiang Yee. New York: The John Day Company, 1953. Permission to reprint granted by Mrs. Gladys Brooks.

The Silent Traveller in Lakeland, the "very holy of holies" of the English nature poets.

The English lake district was a happy field for a Chinese artist with an inborn love of mountains, streams, trees and flowers, and, while he wrote about this region with a singular freshness and lightness of touch, he interpreted it also in pictures and ideograms. Unaccustomed, as he said, to occidental media and techniques, he used his Chinese brushes, inks and colors, following his own native method in painting, and in this and his subsequent travel books, dealing with English and Scottish themes, he produced effects that were equally novel and charming. He was especially fortunate perhaps because England was a land of mists and fogs, like those one saw in so many of the great Chinese paintings, and the fickle English weather pleased him by constantly changing the aspects of scenes while it stirred him to record the changes in his own feelings. With a veil of rain familiar scenes passed through enchanting variations, and even his affection for sunshine increased because it arrived unexpectedly and because, like the objects themselves, it was elusive. He delighted in the soft fresh English green that had, as he remarked, both life in itself and the power of blending other colors, and at every turn the simple things of this countryside that was foreign to him carried his imagination back to China. A group of oaks with twisted trunks or a waterfall on a rugged cliff recalled to his mind's eye some old Sung painting, so that sometimes he followed the Sung style in a picture of his own, and, remembering the poets, hermits, and scholars who had meditated in scenes like these, he was prompted to repeat their sayings and anecdotes about them. He was charmed by a cluster of horses in a meadow, by a heathery hillock, green and blue, fading into gray, melting into the dove-colored sky, by dragonflies clinging to the tops of reeds, a knot of water-lily leaves and buds, a robin or a rose tree in full bloom. Composing a poem now and then, he interspersed his observations with delightful examples of Chinese calligraphy also, with notes on characters whom he had met, wayfaring folk in city streets, old buildings, and the customs of the country.

Mr. Chiang Yee shared Wordsworth's pleasure in the mean-est flower that blows. With none of the clichés of travel-writing, his books possessed the companionable charm of a mind of great natural distinction that was willing to be pleased.

When I heard that the "Silent Traveller" was writing a book about New York, I wondered if he would find this a happy subject. With his fondness for dull rainy days and the misty-moisty English scene, would he like the hard dry light of our stone and steel? In New York he would have for mountain peaks only metallic skyscrapers, and instead of the soft English rain he would have our thoroughly businesslike rain that comes down as if it was also made of steel. I half wished that he had chosen first the luxuriant New England countryside, the valley of the Housatonic, the Franconia mountains, the green hills of Vermont and the foggy, rocky coast of Maine that appears in John Marin's watercolors. What would he not be able to do with the autumn foliage along the rivers or the neatly winning Pal-ladian villages and towns that are surely little known in China? But I had not fully realized the depth of Mr. Chiang Yee's interest in the urban and human as well as the natural scene; and, besides, there were days in New York when clouds enveloped the tall buildings, suggesting for him a Sung painting of high Chinese peaks. In the six months that he spent in the city, he made discoveries in Greenwich Village that will surprise even the oldest New Yorkers, and he made discoveries in Chinatown that surprised a Chinese, for almost everything he heard there was invented for tour-ists. He was alertly curious enough to get up at five on Sun-day morning to see what was left of Times Square after Saturday night; he walked across the George Washington bridge; he sailed up the Hudson to Poughkeepsie; he inves-tigated the Bowery, Broadway, Wall Street, Harlem. He found children everywhere who were lovable and playful. He delighted in the balletlike gestures of the hands and arms of a crowd of girls at the summit of the Empire State Building, from which Central Park looked like a small lacquer tea tray inlaid with jade to represent trees and lakes.

Seen from this height, the other buildings were like infinitesimal bambooshoots in a Chinese grove in early spring. Mr. Chiang Yee's pen-and-ink drawings of street scenes suggest the omnivorous and humorous eye with which he absorbed the multitudinous life of the city, while the parks and botanical gardens of Manhattan and Brooklyn provided for the landscape artist a variety of themes. There he found cherry trees in blossom and willows with branches tossing in the wind that stirred him to write poems as he painted and drew them, and even the natural rock formations, the waterfalls, thickets and gorges that were immemorial subjects of Chinese painters. There were the squirrels with sparkling eyes that were also cherished in Chinese art, and he found birds in every corner of the city. Almost every one of his pictures contains a pigeon, a swan, a crane, or wild geese, ducks, or seagulls flying aloft.

The fact is that Mr. Chiang Yee is a true citizen of the world, like Goldsmith's observer from China, everywhere at home, interested in all things human as well as in animals, trees, and birds, who has given us a fresh New York that is different from all others. An American admirer can only hope that he will visit other regions—Concord, perhaps, and Walden Pond where Confucius and Mencius found wise readers who had the Chinese feeling for Shan-Shui also. Mr. Chiang Yee recalls Thoreau when he says that "winter clears the head," and a Chinese painter in monochrome would find he had much in common with Thoreau, who loved the winter colors of the scrub oak and the rabbit. There are the Carolinas too where Audubon spent happy months among the scenes of William Bartram's *Travels*, the charming book that suggested to Wordsworth and Coleridge some of the famous images that appeared in their poems. Mr. Chiang Yee would find there the azaleas that "set the hills on fire" in *Ruth*, the rhododendrons he always associates with China and the flowering magnolia trees that he knew as a child; and if he went to the Southwest he would find the American Indians who were anciently connected, as he remarks, with his own honorable race. If Mr. Chiang Yee were to read Mrs. Mabel Dodge Luhan's *Winter in Taos*, he might well wish to fly or even walk there. Taos was the "only place that actually realized" for Leo Stein "the vision of the great Chinese landscape painters."

Since I am quoting Leo Stein, I may add what he said of appreciation, which had, he felt, a great role to play in the world. He saw society at the end of a road with only two alternatives, universal war or more appreciation—the appreciation of life and men that would lead people to give up the resistances and repressions that must otherwise lead them to fight. This, as it seems to me, is Mr. Chiang Yee's counsel too, and perhaps the general counsel of Chinese wisdom, one that we should welcome in America, where sanity is the last thing that anyone looks for at present. Mr. Chiang Yee repeats the saying of Mencius that a wise man should retain his childlike mind—a rebuke to our tiresome ideal of "sophistication"; and he says that in securing the freedoms from ignorance and want we should also plan for a "freedom from too many desires." That might be his reply to our foolish cult of advertising, which exists for the breeding of desires, the more the better. In saying that man is a greedy creature, greedy for wealth, food, clothes, or fame, he suggests that he himself is more often greedy for things that delight the eye or delight the mind—that he is appreciative, in short, as he kindles in others the appreciative feeling that alone perhaps can keep the world at peace.

Selected Bibliography

Principal Works of Van Wyck Brooks

The Wine of the Puritans: A Study of Present-Day America.
London: Sisley's, 1908.

*The Malady of the Ideal: Senancour, Maurice de Guérin,
and Amiel.* London: A. C. Fifield, 1913.

John Addington Symonds: A Biographical Study. London:
Mitchell Kenerley, 1914.

The World of H. G. Wells. London: Mitchell Kennerley,
1914.

America's Coming-of-Age. New York: B. W. Huebsch,
1915.

Letters and Leadership. New York: B. W. Huebsch, 1918.

The Ordeal of Mark Twain. New York: E. P. Dutton & Co.,
1920.

History of a Literary Radical: Essays by Randolph Bourne,
ed. by Van Wyck Brooks. New York: B. W. Huebsch,
1920.

The Pilgrimage of Henry James. New York: E. P. Dutton &
Co., 1925.

The American Caravan, ed. by Van Wyck Brooks, Alfred
Kreymborg, Lewis Mumford and Paul Rosenfeld. New
York: The Macauley Company, 1927.

Emerson and Others. New York: E. P. Dutton & Co., 1927.

Sketches in Criticism. New York: E. P. Dutton & Co., 1932.

The Life of Emerson. New York: E. P. Dutton & Co., 1932.

The Journal of Gamaliel Bradford, 1883–1932, ed. by Van
Wyck Brooks. Boston and New York: Houghton Mifflin,
1933.

Three Essays on America. New York: E. P. Dutton & Co.,
1934.

The Flowering of New England, 1915–1865. New York: E. P. Dutton & Co., 1936.

New England: Indian Summer, 1865–1915. New York: E. P. Dutton & Co., 1940.

Opinions of Oliver Allston. New York: E. P. Dutton & Co., 1941.

Roots of American Culture and Other Essays by Constance Rourke, ed. by Van Wyck Brooks. New York: Harcourt, Brace, 1942.

The World of Washington Irving. New York: E. P. Dutton & Co., 1944.

The Times of Melville and Whitman. New York: E. P. Dutton & Co., 1947.

A Chilmark Miscellany. New York: E. P. Dutton & Co., 1948.

The Confident Years, 1885–1915. New York: E. P. Dutton & Co., 1952.

The Writer in America. New York: E. P. Dutton & Co., 1952.

Scenes and Portraits: Memories of Childhood and Youth. New York: E. P. Dutton & Co., 1954.

John Sloan: A Painter's Life. New York: E. P. Dutton & Co., 1955.

Helen Keller: Sketch for a Portrait. New York: E. P. Dutton & Co., 1956.

Days of the Phoenix: The Nineteen-Twenties I Remember. New York: E. P. Dutton & Co., 1957.

Dream of Arcadia: American Writers and Artists in Italy, 1760–1915. New York: E. P. Dutton & Co., 1958.

From a Writer's Notebook. New York: E. P. Dutton & Co., 1958.

Howells: His Life and World. New York: E. P. Dutton & Co., 1959.

From the Shadow of the Mountain: My Post-Meridian Years. New York: E. P. Dutton & Co., 1961.

Fenollosa and His Circle, with Other Essays in Biography. New York: E. P. Dutton & Co., 1962.

Writers at Work: The Paris Review Interviews, Second Series, introduction by Van Wyck Brooks. New York: The Viking Press, 1963.

The Van Wyck Brooks—Lewis Mumford Letters, ed. by Robert E. Spiller. New York: E. P. Dutton & Co., 1970.

Principal Essays in Criticism

Angoff, Charles. "Van Wyck Brooks: A Career in Retrospect," *The Literary Review*, 7:27–35 (Autumn 1963).

Cargill, Oscar. "The Ordeal of Van Wyck Brooks," *College English*, 8:55–61 (November 1946).

Collins, Seward. "Criticism in America: The Origins of a Myth," *Bookman*, 71:241–56; 353–64 (June 1930).

Colum, Mary. "An American Critic: Van Wyck Brooks," *Dial*, 76:33–40 (January 1924).

Cowley, Malcolm. "Van Wyck Brooks: A Career in Retrospect," *Saturday Review*, 46:17–18; 38 (May 25, 1963).

Dupee, F. W. "The Americanism of Van Wyck Brooks," *Partisan Review*. Reprinted in William Phillips and Philip Rahv, eds., *The Partisan Reader*, New York: The Dial Press, 1946.

Foerster, Norman. "The Literary Prophets," *Bookman*, 72:35–44 (September 1930).

Glicksberg, Charles I. "Van Wyck Brooks," *Sewanee Review*, 43:175–86 (April–June 1935).

Hyman, Stanley E. "Van Wyck Brooks and Biographical Criticism," in *The Armed Vision*, New York: Alfred A. Knopf, 1948.

Jones, Howard M. "The Pilgrimage of Van Wyck Brooks," *Virginia Quarterly Review* 8:439–42 (July 1932).

Kenton, Edna, "Henry James and Mr. Van Wyck Brooks," *Bookman*, 42:153–57 (October 1925).

Kohler, Dayton. "Van Wyck Brooks: Traditionally American," *College English*, 2:629–39 (April 1941).

Leary, Lewis. "Standing with Reluctant Feet," in *A Casebook on Mark Twain's Wound*, New York: Thomas Y. Crowell, 1962.

Leavis, F. R. "The Americanness of American Literature," in *Anna Karenina and Other Essays*, New York: Pantheon Books, 1967.

Maynard, Theodore. "Van Wyck Brooks," *Catholic World*, 140:412–21 (January 1935).

Morrison, Claudia C. "Van Wyck Brooks's Analysis of Mark Twain," *Freud and the Critic*, Chapel Hill: University of North Carolina Press, 1968.

Munson, Gorham B. "Van Wyck Brooks: His Sphere and His Encroachments," *Dial*, 78:28–42 (January 1925).

Rosenfeld, Paul. "Van Wyck Brooks," *Port of New York*, New York: Harcourt, Brace, 1924; Urbana: University of Illinois Press, 1961.

Smith, Bernard. "Van Wyck Brooks," in Malcolm Cowley, ed., *After the Genteel Tradition*. New York: W. W. Norton & Co., 1937; Carbondale: Southern Illinois University Press, 1964.

Wade, John D. "The Flowering of New England," *Southern Review*, 2:807–14 (Fall 1937).

Wellek, René. "Van Wyck Brooks and a National Literature," *American Prefaces*, 7:292–306 (Summer 1942).

Wescott, Glenway. "Van Wyck Brooks," *The New York Times Book Review*, 2 (December 13, 1965).

Wilson, Edmund. "Imaginary Conversations: Mr. F. Scott Fitzgerald and Mr. Van Wyck Brooks," *New Republic*, 38:249–54 (April 30, 1924). Reprinted in *The Shores of Light*. New York: Farrar, Straus and Young, 1952.

Index

Aaron, Daniel, 5. *See also* Dupee, F. W.; Schwartz, Delmore

Adams, Brooks, 97

Adams, Henry, 29, 62, 95–97, 100, 103, 111

—*Democracy*, 95–97, *Education of Henry Adams, The*, 95; *Esther*, 96; *History of the United States During the Administration of Jefferson and Madison*, 95; *Mont-Saint-Michel and Chartres*, 95

Adams, J. Donald: as eulogist of Brooks, 5

Addison, Joseph, 82

Adler, Alfred, 43, 44. *See also* Hart, Bernard

Aiken, Conrad, 29. *See also* Expatriation

American Academy of Arts and Letters, 9, 76, 80

American grain, 65, 66–67, 69, 72, 77

America's Coming-of-Age: "The American Myth" as Brook's choice for subtitle of, 39*n*

Amiel, Henri Frédéric, 2, 23, 24, 27, 48, 73, 132

Anderson, Sherwood: Brooks's influence on, 3

Angoff, Charles, 5

Anthropomorphism, 65. *See also* Huizinga, Johan

Antiurbanism: *Makers and Finders* interpreted as, 72

Archer, Isabel: resemblance to Helen Keller, 11

Arnold, Matthew, 28

Artzybasheff, Mikhail, 106. *See also* Howells, William Dean

Arvin, Newton, 74. *See also* Matthiessen, F. O.; Radicalism, literary

Ashcan painters, 17, 107–8. *See also* Yeats, John Butler

Atkinson, Brooks: as eulogist of Brooks, 5

Atlantic Monthly, The: Howells's editorship of, 102

Audubon, John James, 83, 139. *See also* Yee, Chiang

Babbitt, Irving, 2, 13. *See also* More, Paul Elmer; Mencken, H. L.

Balzac, Honoré de, 87. *See also* Cooper, James Fenimore

Bartram, William: *Travels*, 139. *See also* Yee, Chiang

Baudelaire, Charles: Howells's reference to, 107

Beecher, Lyman, 91, 92. *See*